# THE PERFECT
# COVER LETTER

# THE PERFECT COVER LETTER

RICHARD H. BEATTY

WILEY

**JOHN WILEY & SONS**

New York • Chichester • Brisbane • Toronto • Singapore

This publication is designed to provide accurate and
authoritative information in regard to the subject
matter covered. It is sold with the understanding that
the publisher is not engaged in rendering legal, accounting,
or other professional service. If legal advice or other
expert assistance is required, the services of a competent
professional person should be sought. *From a Declaration
of Principles jointly adopted by a Committee of the
American Bar Association and a Committee of Publishers.*

Library of Congress Cataloging-in-Publication Data

Beatty, Richard H., 1939–
  The perfect cover letter.

  Bibliography: p.
  1. Résumés (Employment)  2. Cover letters.  I. Title.
HF5383.B325  1989          650.1'4        88-33797
ISBN 0471-50202-2
ISBN 0471-50203-0 (pbk.)

Printed in the United States of America

20  19  18  17  16  15  14  13  12

To all those who agonize over
the chore of letter writing.

# PREFACE

Curiously, most job seekers invest considerable time and effort in preparing the ultimate resume; however, few invest nearly the same amount of care in preparing the employment cover letter—the very document that first introduces them to a prospective employer. As a seasoned employment professional, I have always found this an interesting phenomenon—one that I intend to address in this book.

Much has been written on the importance of first impressions to the success of the interview. We have all been led to believe that the impression created by the employment candidate during the first few minutes of the interview will have significant impact on the outcome. If this impression is positive, the candidate's chances for employment are substantially enhanced. Conversely, if it is negative, an unfavorable outcome is all but guaranteed!

But what about the cover letter? Doesn't this document, in most cases, serve as the employment candidate's first contact with the employer? Isn't it possible that it can also have some very real impact on the initial impressions (good or bad) that the employer will have of the candidate? Unquestionably, the answer to these questions is an emphatic "Yes!"

I clearly believe that the cover letter can have a significant impact on the outcome of the employment process. If well-written, it can create excitement and interest in your employment candidacy. If poorly written, it can prove absolutely fatal to an otherwise well-planned and well-orchestrated job search campaign.

It is well known that the cover letter can prove very insightful to employment professionals. Actually, most are known to use this document to make observations about such important factors as:

1. Written communication skills
2. Organization skills
3. Overall intelligence
4. Overall focus and priorities
5. Personal style
6. Social skills
7. Business or management philosophy, or both
8. Operating style
9. Management style
10. Technical knowledge

Clearly, then, the overall design, content, and construction of the employment cover letter can play a major role in the effectiveness of your job hunting campaign. With so much riding on it, it is important, therefore, to commit the necessary time and effort to this too-often-ignored, but critical, element of the job search program.

Considering the importance of cover letters, it is surprising to me that so little has been written on the subject. To my knowledge, this is the only book that focuses exclusively on this critical topic. In my opinion, it is a book that is long overdue.

The purpose of this book, therefore, is to provide you with a practical "hands-on" manual for design and construction of highly effective cover letters that enhance and support your job search objectives. Its emphasis is on practical application. Material is presented in a logical, step-by-step manner to facilitate the writing process.

The book begins by discussing the purpose and importance of cover letters and contrasts good and poor cover letter design. It then proceeds through the advance preparation steps needed to put the right information at your fingertips. A chapter is included that gives practical advice concerning the kinds of information that should be included in the cover letter and those best left out. The final four chapters provide detailed instructions for preparing a wide range of cover and employment letters, and contain numerous examples of such letters for your easy reference.

By following the advice provided in this book, and by using the sample cover letters as models, you should be well-equipped to write interesting letters that prove very additive to your job hunting campaign.

Happy writing, and best wishes to you for a highly successful employment campaign!

RICHARD H. BEATTY

*West Chester, Pennsylvania*
*February 1989*

# CONTENTS

# 1

# AN INTRODUCTION TO COVER LETTERS

The cover letter that accompanies your employment résumé is perhaps one of the most important letters you will ever write. Other than your résumé, it is the single key document that will introduce you to a prospective employer and, if well-written, pave the way to that all-important job interview. It is an integral part of your overall job hunting campaign, and it can make or break you, depending upon how well it is written. Construction of this document should therefore be given very careful attention. The care that you give to writing this letter will certainly be a major factor in getting your job search off to an excellent start. Conversely, a poorly written letter will surely scuttle your campaign before it even begins.

## The Purpose of the Cover Letter

Before you can expect to write an effective cover letter, you must understand its purpose. Without a clear understanding of what this letter is intended to accomplish, chances are it will be poorly designed, vague, and totally ineffective. On the other hand, understanding the purpose of this letter is truly paramount to maximizing its impact and effectiveness.

What is the purpose of the cover letter? What is it intended to do?

Well, first and foremost, it is a business letter used to transmit your résumé to a prospective employer. So, it is a business transmittal letter. Second, it is a letter of introduction. It is used not only to transmit your résumé but also to introduce you and your background to the employer. Third, and importantly, it is a sales letter, intended to convince the prospective employer that you have something valuable to contribute and that it will be worth the employer's time to grant you an interview.

To summarize, then, the purpose of a cover letter is:

1. To serve as a business transmittal letter for your résumé.
2. To introduce you and your employment credentials to the employer.
3. To generate employer interest in interviewing you.

Certainly, knowing that these are the three main objectives of a well-written cover letter will provide you with some basic starting points. We will be further discussing these objectives and the related elements of good design throughout this book. For now, it is important to simply keep these objectives in mind as we further explore the topic of effective cover letters.

## From the Employer's Prospective

When contemplating good cover letter design and construction, it is important to keep one very important fact in mind: The cover letter must be written from the employer's perspective.

Stated differently, good cover letter writing must take into consideration that the end result you seek is employer action. More specifically, you want the employer to grant you an interview, so it is important to understand those factors that will motivate an employer to do so. To understand this important phenomenon, it is necessary to realistically address the following questions:

1.  How does the employer read the cover letter?
2.  What are the key factors the employer is looking for (and expects to find) in the cover letter?
3.  What are the motivational factors that will pique the employer's curiosity and create a desire to interview you?

I think you will agree that these are some very important questions to ask if you are to be successful in designing cover letters that will be truly helpful to your job hunting program. You must pay close attention to the needs of the prospective employer, rather than just your own, if you expect to write cover letters that will motivate him or her to take action. Cover letters must, therefore, be "employer focused" rather than "job searcher focused" if you want to really maximize their overall effectiveness.

Top sales producers have always known that the most important principle in sales success, whether selling goods or services, is selling to the needs of the buyer. What is the customer really buying? Where are the priorities? What specific needs does he or she need to satisfy? Without knowing the answers to these questions, it is easy for the salesperson to emphasize product characteristics and attributes that have absolutely no relationship to the customer's real needs, and de-emphasize characteristics and attributes that are truly important. The result—no sale!

In the ideal sense, therefore, it is important to research your target companies very well to determine what it is that they are buying (i.e., looking for in a successful employment candidate). If you are conducting a general broadcast campaign covering several hundred companies, such individual company research may simply not be feasible. If, on the other hand, you are targeting a dozen or so employers for whom you would really like to work, such research is not only feasible but should be considered an "absolute must." Careful advance research, in this case, will pay huge dividends, returning your initial investment of time and effort manyfold.

Even in the case of the general broadcast campaign, where you have targeted several hundred companies, there are clearly some things that you can do to focus your cover letters on the real needs of these employers. Here are some guidelines for conducting meaningful employer needs research:

1. Divide your target list of employers into industry groupings.
2. Using industry trade publications and key newspapers (available in most libraries), thoroughly research each industry grouping for answers to the following questions:

   a. What is the general state of this industry?
   b. What are the major problems faced by companies in this industry?
   c. What are the barriers or roadblocks that stand in the way of solving these problems?
   d. What knowledge, skills, and capabilities are needed to address these problems and roadblocks?
   e. What major trends and changes are being driven by companies in this industry?
   f. What new knowledge, skills, and capabilities are needed to successfully drive these changes and trends?

Having conducted this research, you are now in a position to better focus your cover letter on key needs areas of interest to the majority of companies in each of your targeted industry groupings. This provides you with the opportunity to showcase your overall knowledge, skills, and capabilities in relation to those important needs areas. Such focusing substantially increases your chances for hitting the employer's bull's-eye, which will result in job interviews.

Where you can narrow your list to a dozen or so key companies, individual company research can have even greater payoff. Here, you have the opportunity to really zero in on the specific needs of the employer, and you can bring into play a number of research techniques for doing so. The research you do here can, in fact, be tailored to each individual firm; so you can substantially increase your probability of success and up by quite a bit the number of potential interview opportunities.

In many ways, the methodology used in conducting single-firm research is similar to that already described for industry-wide research. You will note some of these similarities as you review the following guidelines for researching the single firm.

1. Determine the firms you would like to target for individual research (firms for which you would really like to work).

2. Using industry trade publications and key newspapers (available at your local library) as well as annual reports, 10K forms, and product literature (available from the target firm's public affairs and marketing departments), thoroughly research for answers to the following questions:

   a. What is the general state of the company?
   b. How does it stack up against competition?
   c. What are the key problems and issues with which it is currently wrestling?
   d. What are the key barriers that must be removed in order to resolve these problems/issues?
   e. What knowledge, skills, and capabilities are needed to remove these key barriers?
   f. What are the company's strategic goals?
   g. What are the key changes that will need to come about for realization of these goals?
   h. What new knowledge, skills, and capabilities will be needed to bring about these critical changes?

Here, as with research of industry groupings, individual company research enables you to use the cover letter to highlight your knowledge, skills, and capabilities in areas that are of importance to the firm. In the case of individual firm research, however, there is the added advantage of being able to tailor the cover letter to target your qualifications to very specific, known needs of the employer. This can provide you with a substantial competitive advantage!

Another technique that you should employ when doing individual firm research is networking. If you don't already belong, you might consider joining specific industry or professional associations to which employees of your individual target firms belong. Using your common membership in these organizations as the basis, you can call these employees for certain inside information. Here are some questions you might consider asking:

1. Is the firm hiring people in your functional specialty?
2. Are there openings in this group now?
3. Who within the company is the key line manager (i.e., outside human resources) responsible for hiring for this group?
4. What are the key things this manager tends to look for in a successful candidate (e.g., technical knowledge, skills, style, etc.)?
5. What key problems/issues is the group currently wrestling with?
6. What kinds of skills and capabilities are they looking for to address these issues?
7. What are the major strategic changes this group is attempting to drive?
8. What qualifications and attributes is the group seeking to help them drive these strategic changes?

Obviously, answers to these questions can give you a tremendous competitive advantage when designing an effective cover letter and employment résumé. You will have substantial ammunition for targeting and highlighting those qualifications of greatest interest to the employer. Here, you can make the most of your opportunity for successful self-marketing by focusing on the critical needs not only of the organization but of the functional hiring group as well. Clearly, this is a technique you should employ if you want to maximize your chances of getting hired!

The underlying principle behind this needs research methodology, whether industry grouping or individual company research, is that organizations are always looking for individuals who will be "value adding"—that is, individuals who can help them solve key problems and realize strategic objectives. These are the candidates who are seen as the value-adding change agents—the leaders who will help move the company ahead rather than cause it to stand still. Employer needs research will allow you to design effective cover letters that can truly set you apart from the competition and substantially improve your chances for landing interviews.

## How Cover Letters Are Read

Although, in many cases, it can be clearly self-defeating, the great majority of résumés and accompanying cover letters are sent to the attention of the employment or personnel department. It is here that the cover letter probably least serves the interests of the job seeker.

The truth of the matter is that most personnel and employment professionals are unlikely to pay much real attention to the cover letter. In the course of a year, it is estimated that the employment manager of a medium- to large-size company may read over 20,000 résumés along with accompanying cover letters. This considerable experience has led most professionals to conclude that cover letters add little meaningful information to that already provided in the résumé itself. Such letters are usually of the "broadcast" variety and are frequently redundant to the résumé.

Having learned this, the employment or personnel manager will normally give the cover letter only a cursory glance and concentrate on reading the résumé itself, since this is the document that details the specifics of the candidate's background and qualifications and that is used for comparing these qualifications with the candidate specification of the position that the manager is trying to fill.

When reading the cover letter, the employment manager is usually looking to see if it is the mass-mailed "broadcast" kind, or if it is more personal or specific to the company. Managers usually try to ferret out letters that indicate any kind of firsthand association with the company—for example, friends of employees and executives, shareholders, and local community leaders. These letters normally require a more personal response, and care is taken so that an inappropriate form response is not accidentally sent. Unfortunately, however, cover letters of a less personal nature normally receive very little attention from employment/personnel professionals.

If this is the case, then why write a book on cover letters? Why take time to provide advice to people on how to best design and construct such letters if they are barely read? The answer to this is fairly simple.

I am recommending that, in most cases, you not send your cover letter and résumé to the personnel and employment departments of the firms that you have targeted for your mailing. Instead, I am strongly recommending, where at all possible, that you address your correspondence to a specific individual within the corporation. This person should be at a fairly high level and should be within the particular business function or discipline most closely related to the position for which you are applying. Thus, if you are a tax accountant, you will want to direct your letter to the director of taxes. Similarly, if you are an engineering manager, you will want to write to either the director or vice president of engineering. If you are already at the director or vice president level, however, you should correspond with the firm's president or chief operating officer.

What is the logic behind my recommendation to send your cover letter and résumé directly to the line function rather than the personnel department? Again, the answer is fairly simple. I certainly have no hostility toward human resources professionals and recognize that many are highly competent. The reason for my recommendation is that the employment manager, in many cases, has knowledge only of those positions that are currently open. He or she may be totally unaware of the future hiring needs of line managers—needs that they are thinking about filling at some future point. In some cases, "some future point" can be as immediate as next week or next month. A well-written cover letter accompanying a résumé may be just the thing that causes the hiring executive to move ahead and fill the position now.

A line manager will usually read the cover letter a little more thoroughly than will the employment manager. The motivation is different. The employment manager is simply looking for credentials that match a current open position, whereas the line manager (the one who does the actual hiring) is looking for solutions to existing problems; new ideas for bringing improvement to the organization; understanding of new, emerging business concepts and trends; and so forth. In general, this manager is looking for ways to add value to the organization. He or she will thus tend to read the cover letter and résumé more closely, with a view toward addressing the aforementioned need categories. Your well-constructed cover letter and résumé may suggest that you can help to address these needs—that you are someone who could add real value to the organization. The result could well be an invitation for an employment interview.

Here again is further argument in favor of the points made earlier in this chapter about the importance of target company needs research. If, through good research, you can pinpoint the specific problems, trends, and strategic objectives of this employer, you have a much better basis for constructing a highly focused cover letter that addresses them. If your specific knowledge and qualifications suggest that you may have some good answers, and you have highlighted this in your cover letter, you have created what is known in economics as the "accelerator effect" and have increased the probability of an employment interview manyfold.

In summary, the way a cover letter is written should directly relate to the way it will likely be read. Where possible, through good advance research (either by industry grouping or by individual firm), it should be designed to highlight your qualifications to solve contemporary problems, facilitate current trends, apply state-of-the-art methodology, and drive desired strategic change. To maximize effectiveness, your letter must convey a sense that you are a person who will be adding value in those key areas where the target company is looking for answers and desires improvement.

Your cover letters thus need to be "reader aligned" rather than "writer aligned." They must address the real needs of the prospective employer, not just your needs. The key to such alignment is advance research, without which your letters will be like buckshot in a strong wind rather than a well-aimed single shot directed at the center of the bull's eye. It is likely to miss the target and cripple an otherwise well-planned job search process.

## The Advantages of a Good Cover Letter

This chapter has, I hope, served to increase your awareness of the importance of a good cover letter to your job hunting campaign. Let's explore this topic in greater depth, however, so that you can more fully appreciate its importance.

Starting at the beginning, it is important to realize that the employment cover letter is, in most cases, the very first contact that you have with the employer, who reads it before he or she even begins to look at your résumé. The important thing to realize here is that if the letter is poorly written, many employers may never even bother to go as far as to read your résumé; it can be an automatic turnoff, leading the employer to move on to the next cover letter and résumé. A poor cover letter can screen you out of the employment selection process before you even get started. You may never have an opportunity to compete.

The appearance of the cover letter, as with the résumé, makes a personal statement about you to the prospective employer. If it is ill-conceived, disorganized, and sloppy, it will suggest that you are disorganized and sloppy in your work. It may also suggest that you don't care about the impression you make on others and that you are not particularly well motivated. Likewise, if the cover letter rambles and lacks focus, it may suggest that you are verbose and nonfocused and generally lack a sense of organization.

By contrast, a well-planned, well-written, highly focused cover letter will make quite a different statement about you to a prospective employer. It will suggest that you are very thorough and careful, and that you take a great deal of pride in your work. It may also suggest that you are well-organized, strategic, focused, and results-oriented. Thus, there is a decided upgrade to your job hunting campaign through the employment of well-planned, well-designed cover letters that create a highly favorable impression.

Besides a favorable image, a good cover letter also provides you with an excellent vehicle to highlight key aspects of your credentials that are closely related to major needs of the prospective employer. In this sense, if well-written and properly focused, it can do a much better job of selling your value to a prospective employer than can the accompanying résumé, which leaves the employer with the challenge of wandering through a maze of information to ferret out those qualifications that are truly relevant to his or her contemporary needs. The cover letter can thus become an extremely forceful sales tool for persuading the employer that a job interview would be a very worthwhile investment.

It cannot be overemphasized that the effectiveness of the cover letter as a sales tool is directly related to the quality of your advance research on the real needs of the firms on your target list. Although well-organized and well-written, if your cover letter fails to focus on the major needs of the employer, a substantial opportunity to maximize its sales effectiveness is lost, and the direct result will likely be substantially reduced interview opportunities.

It's up to you, then, to make the cover letter what it can be—a significant enhancement to your job hunting campaign or a negative drain that casts you in a poor light and substantially detracts from your access to excellent job and career opportunities. The choice is yours!

The ensuing chapters will provide you with the help you will need to plan, construct, and write cover letters that are targeted to the needs of employers and that maximize your opportunities for employment interviews—the perfect cover letter, so to speak.

# 2

# COVER LETTER FORMAT

Writing a successful cover letter will require that you use a proper business letter format—one that is widely used and accepted for this purpose. It is, therefore, important that you familiarize yourself with those letter formats that are most commonly used and recognized as acceptable for cover letters.

By "format," I mean the actual design and physical layout of the letter. This is different from the "content" of the letter, which means the topics and matter discussed in the text. This chapter will deal with the subject of proper letter format. The subject of content (what should be included in or excluded from the cover letter) will be dealt with in considerable depth in the ensuing chapters of this book.

### The Importance of Format

The physical layout and design of a cover letter is important to its effectiveness for several reasons.

First, good layout and design enhance appearance and serve to create a favorable impression on the part of the reader. A letter that is well-designed, properly spaced, and neat will create a positive image of you as an individual. It will suggest to prospective employers that you are logical, neat, and well-organized. Conversely, an improperly or poorly designed letter can convey just the opposite and thus leave a negative impression.

Second, a neat, concise, and well-organized format will substantially improve readability and thereby enhance communications and increase the probability that your cover letter it will be read. Additionally, a good format will properly highlight the important aspects of your credentials, thus improving the chances of successfully marketing yourself to prospective employers.

Third, failure to employ an acceptable business letter format may suggest that you are ignorant of common business practices or, worse, that you simply don't care. Neither impression will help your cause and may, in fact, detract substantially from your self-marketing efforts and your overall job hunting plan.

It should be evident from this discussion that using an acceptable cover letter format is important to your job search. Therefore, you should be sufficiently motivated to follow the advice offered in this chapter.

## Acceptable Letter Format

A random sampling of several hundred cover letters received by our executive search practice during the last few months suggests that there are three acceptable formats commonly used by job seekers in the preparation of their employment cover letters. These three formats and their respective percents of usage, as determined by this survey, are shown below.

| *Type of Cover Letter Format* | *Percent Used* |
| --- | --- |
| Full Block | 49% |
| Block | 34% |
| Modified Block | 17% |

In reviewing the results of this survey, it is important to note that virtually 100 percent of the cover letters received by our executive search firm utilized only three formats. And since the only basic difference between the block and the modified block format is that the latter utilizes paragraph indentation, there are actually only two basic letter formats acceptable for the employment cover letter. These are the full block and the block/modified block versions.

If the overwhelming practice among job seekers is to use one of these two designs, common sense indicates that these formats must have something going for them, and that departure from them is likely to result in an aberration that might jeopardize your cover letter's effectiveness.

Some would argue that in cover letter preparation, as in résumé preparation, you should "dare to be different." The usual argument here is that the unconventional format stands out from the pack and thus compels reading. Those of you who might be somewhat swayed by this logic are encouraged to think more broadly about the issue.

The assumption is that the unconventional design not only compels attention but also suggests to prospective employers that you are a creative and resourceful individual who will contribute new ideas and fresh thinking to the organization. Are you convinced? Although the logic is impeccable, the reality of the end result can spell a job hunting disaster of the first order. You've heard the saying that one man's junk is another man's treasure? How about the saying that beauty is in the eye of the beholder? The point here is that there are differences in human perception. Actually, what you feel is a clever, creative approach that sets you apart from the hordes may, in the eyes of the prospective employer, automatically classify you as a nonconforming, maladjusted, antisocial person, ignorant of acceptable business practice, immature, foolish, idiotic, or something else less than complimentary.

When it comes to designing your cover letter, my best advice is to leave creativity to the artists and stick with proven, time-tested approaches that will effectively promote your employment credentials and thus enhance your prospects of landing an interview. I have read thousands of cover letters and résumés, and I can assure you that your interests will be much better served by sticking with common business practice. I have seen many attempts at cleverness, creativity, or humor fall far short of the author's intended mark and substantially detract from an otherwise effective employment presentation. Why take the chance?

We will use the rest of this chapter to thoroughly familiarize you with the two most common cover letter formats—the full block and the block/modified block. Each of these will be described in detail and illustrated by examples. First, however, it will be necessary to discuss the standard components of the business letter so that their nomenclature will be clearly understood.

## Components of the Cover Letter

The standard components of a cover letter, in the order in which they are positioned in the actual letter, are: return address, date, address, salutation, body, complimentary closing, signature, typist identification, and enclosure line. Although seldom used, some additional, optional components are: attention line, subject line, copy line, and postscript. Let's examine each of these components for correct positioning, usage, content, and punctuation. Proper use of these components is paramount to correct cover letter design and format.

### Return Address

The return address is the address to which you wish return correspondence directed. In the case of the employment cover letter, this is normally the address of your residence. In certain cases, it could be the address of your current employer, if your employer is aware of your job search. Use of a business address is generally discouraged, however, since this can create some doubt concerning the reasons for such open-

ness; for example, are you being involuntarily terminated for poor performance?

The following are examples of return addresses:

125 East Warrington Street
West Chester, PA 19382

Apartment # 325
Windham Gate Apartments
Post Road at Surrey Place
Waterford Leas, MA 25118

P.O. Box 235
Burlington, VT 87246

Close examination and comparison of these examples will reveal some
common characteristics, as follows:

1.  The first letter or numeral of each line is directly aligned with
    the first letter or numeral of the preceding line. No lines are
    indented.
2.  The first line is the specific location: number and street address,
    apartment number, post office box number, etc.
3.  Each succeeding line moves from a more specific to a more
    general location (e.g., Apartment # 325, to Post Road at Surrey
    Place, to Waterford Leas, MA).
4.  The final line of the return address contains the name of the
    town or city, state, and postal zip code.
5.  Each word of the address starts with a capital letter.
6.  The name of the town or city is followed by a comma.
7.  The name of the state is abbreviated, using the Postal Service
    abbreviation, and is followed by the appropriate Postal zip code.

The positioning of the return address on the page, determined by the
type of letter format chosen (full block or block/modified block), is
discussed later in this chapter. Depending upon the length of the letter,
however, the first line of the return address is normally positioned
between 6 to 10 lines from the top of the page. Additionally, all lines
comprising the return address are single-spaced.

## *Date*

Obviously, the date shown on the cover letter is the actual date on which the letter is written. This date is positioned on the very next line below the return address and is aligned so that the first letter or numeral of the date is directly in line with the first letter of the return address line that precedes it.

The date is usually displayed in a month–day–year sequence. The first letter of the month is always capitalized, and the name of the month is spelled out in full—never abbreviated. Thus, the following is an example of a correct date:

March 3, 1995

The day of the month is, of course, always followed by a comma.

Although not as commonly used in the cover letter, a day–month–year sequence is also acceptable business practice. Thus, the following example would be considered acceptable practice:

3 March 1995

In this case, the order of the dateline is day, month (the first letter of which is capitalized), and year. There is no punctuation used in this format.

Although acceptable business practice, the day–month–year date sequence is normally used for business-to-business correspondence. It is also commonly used in military and other government correspondence. Generally, this form of correspondence is considered to be more formal than the cover letter, which is actually a more personal type of correspondence (i.e., individual writing to organization rather than organization writing to organization). For this reason, I much prefer and recommend the month–day–year sequence—the format commonly associated with personal correspondence. In my judgment, it allows you to come across as personal and sincere rather than formal or stuffy. In most cases, I believe, this approach will tend to create a closer personal bond with the reader and thereby better serve your interests.

### *Address*

The address is the address of the organization to which you are sending your cover letter. This component comprises the addressee's name and title, the name of the addressee's organization, and the organization's full mailing address.

In both the full block and block/modified block formats, as will be illustrated later in this chapter, the address section is blocked flush with the left margin of the letter. It is also single-spaced, with the first line starting on the next line following the date.

The first line of the address begins with the name of the individual to whom you are writing. Always use his or her full formal name, including middle initial, if known.

Whenever a business letter is addressed to a specific individual, as should always be the case with a good cover letter, the addressee's name should be preceded by a courtesy title (Mr., Ms, Mrs., Dr., etc.). Although no longer an absolute requirement in general business correspondence, the use of the courtesy or social title adds a personal touch to the correspondence, which is lost when only the addressee's name is used. It also connotes a measure of respect for the person as one who will make certain judgments on behalf of his or her organization concerning your employment candidacy.

A word of caution, here, however! The special sensitivities created by the strong desire of most women to be accepted as equals of men in the business world suggest that, in most cases, you should not attempt to distinguish a woman's marital status. As with the use of the social title "Mr.," which has come to designate either a married or unmarried man, the social title "Ms" has come to represent a married or unmarried woman. When addressing a woman in the employment cover letter, therefore, it is recommended that the courtesy title "Ms" be used.

There is only one exception to the use of "Ms" in cover letters addressed to women. In cases where you are personally acquainted with the addressee and you know that she prefers to be addressed as either "Mrs." or "Miss," it is acceptable to use these titles. If you are in doubt concerning this preference, however, I strongly advise using "Ms."

In the case of attorneys and medical doctors, the social title does not precede the addressee's name. Instead, the appropriate title follows the name, as below:

Mary D. Smith, M.D.
John R. Smith, Esq.

Curiously, it has not become practice to use "Esq." when addressing women attorneys. This has to do with the derivation of the word "Esquire," which was historically used by the British as a term of respect for a man (not necessarily a lawyer). Hence, the title of Esquire is never used with a female attorney.

Although in most modern business letters, use of a company or business title is considered optional, it is recommended that such titles be used in the employment cover letter. There are several reasons for this. First, such titles are courteous and convey respect for the person to whom you are writing. Second, the title used (Vice President of Engineering, Director of Manufacturing, etc.) frequently designates the department or function in which you are interested and may thus ensure that your letter gets to the right place in the event of a recent change in personnel. Finally, the title may well serve to jog your memory, at some future point in your job search campaign, if you are trying to remember whether you have written to a specific department within one of your target companies.

The length of the business title will determine whether or not it should be included on the same line as the addressee's name. If it is relatively short, it is fairly common practice to include it on the same line. It is also considered quite acceptable to include the title as a separate line immediately below the name, particularly when the title is a lengthy one. The key here is aesthetics.

Should inclusion of the title on the first line create a noticeable imbalance, move it to the second line (directly beneath the addressee's name). Unless the title is unusually long, it is not considered acceptable practice to split it between two lines. Although not normally recommended, it is advisable in such unusual cases to use some abbreviations in an effort to accommodate the title on a single line.

On the line immediately following the company title, you may want to include the department or function in which the person is employed, unless this function or department is already included in the person's job title. If no such functional or departmental designation is included in the addressee's job title, and you are certain of the exact name, you will probably want to include it as part of the address section of the cover letter. The operative word here is "exact." If you are not sure of the exact name of the department or function, either call the company for verification or leave it out of the address entirely.

In the case where job title is included on the first line of the address along with the addressee's name, the name and title are separated by a comma. In all cases, the first letters of both the job title and department or function are capitalized.

The next line of the address section should show the formal name of the organization. You may elect to use either the company's full formal name or its official abbreviation—for example, either IBM Corporation or International Business Machines Corporation. Although it is generally acceptable to use such abbreviations as "Co.," "Corp.," or "Inc.," follow the company's own practice in this regard. Consult a reputable business directory or the firm's own stationery, if available, for correct spelling and abbreviations.

The street address immediately follows the name of the organization. It normally includes street number, directional quadrant (north, south, east, and west) where appropriate, and street name or title. Street numbers are normally spelled out up to ten; over ten they are represented by numerals. "Street" and "avenue" are not customarily abbreviated; however, "boulevard" is often abbreviated as "Blvd." The first letters of all words in the street address line are capitalized.

If a post office box is used instead of a street address, the common way of writing it is "P.O. Box——." As with the street address, all initial letters are capitalized.

The final line of the address section of the cover letter contains the name of the town or city, the name of the state, and the zip code. The name of the town or city begins with a capital letter and is followed by a comma. The name of the state is abbreviated using the official abbreviation designated by the Postal Service. This is followed by the zip code.

Examples of typical address sections follow:

Mr. William P. Denting, President
The Keller Group
25 North Billings Road
Northfield, MI 66258

Ms Sandra M. Lindstrom
Director of Manufacturing
S.D. Warren Company
118 Enterprise Way
Chicago, IL 28395

Michael F. Davingport, M.D.
Crossworth Medical Institute, Inc.
P.O. Box 345
Kansas City, MO 19472

Ms Katherine R. Lorring, Vice President
Public Affairs Department
Smith, Barnam and Jergeson, Inc.
4215 Worchester Blvd.
Portsmouth, NH 81375

Mr. David Bracksbee, Esq.
President
Bracksbee, Feathersom and Binker, Inc.
Nine Olympic Place
Seattle, WA 99836

### Salutation

The salutation is used to greet the person to whom you are writing. In business letters, if the person to whom you are writing is not personally known, the common practice is to use "Dear," followed by the courtesy or social title (Mr., Ms, Dr., etc.) and then the person's surname. For example:

Dear Ms Wilson:

Dear Dr. Arlingar:

Dear Senator Bacon:

Use of the first name or a nickname in business correspondence, although a growing trend, is not considered appropriate unless you have been personally introduced. Even then, it is important to carefully consider the closeness of the relationship before following this practice in your cover letter. Unless you are already on a first-name basis, it is best not to. This is especially true if the individual to whom you are writing is at a significantly higher level in the organization than you. Use of the first name in such a case could be considered discourteous or inappropriate and could prove fatal to your employment effort.

On the other hand, if you have been introduced on a first-name basis to the addressee, by all means use his or her first name in your correspondence. If this was only a chance meeting, you may need to recall the introduction in the opening paragraph, and the letter will usually need to be written in a more personal tone than that used in the typical broadcast cover letter. The basic principle is that the more personal the tone of your letter, the greater the probability of a personal response.

A subtle reminder of personal connections with the reader will, in almost all cases, substantially improve your chances of an interview and possible employment. Use these personal connections, but don't abuse them.

Although this should rarely happen if you have been thorough in your research, sometimes you may need to address your cover letter to an organizational title or function, without having a specific name. Should you be unable to avoid this particular circumstance, then the salutation will need to be changed accordingly.

Since you will not know the gender of the person to whom you are writing, you will be unable to use the traditional salutation. In such cases, you may wish to use one of the following:

Dear Sir:

Ladies and Gentlemen:

Dear Sir or Madam:

Today, the greeting "Dear Sir" may appear somewhat sexist. For this reason, either of the other two choices is preferred.

In both the full block and block/modified block cover letter formats, the salutation is always placed flush with the left margin and positioned two to four lines below the last line of the address section.

### Body

The body of the cover letter is positioned two lines below the salutation. It contains your message for the addressee. The exact positioning of this message will vary with the type of letter format chosen.

In the full block and block formats, all text, including the first line of each new paragraph, is positioned flush with the left margin. In the modified block format, however, the first line of each new paragraph is indented five spaces from the left margin.

The text of both medium-length and long letters is single-spaced, with double-spacing used to separate paragraphs. Although short quotations should be contained in the normal flow of text and separated by quotation marks, lengthy quotations (usually those exceeding 50 words) are completely set off from the text, in a single-spaced block with double spacing above and below the block. These longer quotations are also normally indented five spaces from both margins.

When the cover letter contains lists or enumerations, these are formatted similarly to lengthy quotations. Normally, such lists are treated as a block of text and separated from the regular text by double-spacing above and below. As with the long quotation, the items contained in the list are indented five spaces from both margins. List items that occupy more than one line of text are single-spaced, with double-spacing separating each complete item.

We will not attempt to cover the content of the cover letter body at this point, since it is the subject of a good portion of this book and will vary depending upon the kind of cover letter written.

### Complimentary Closing

The complimentary closing is the word grouping used to bring the message or text to a close. It is positioned immediately following the body of the letter and just preceding the author's signature. The exact position depends upon the letter format chosen and is explained fully later in this chapter. Normal spacing between the last line of body text and the complimentary closing, however, is usually two spaces.

The complimentary closing you choose should bear some relationship to your familiarity with the reader. "Yours," "Best regards," "Regards," "Best wishes," and so forth, are considered somewhat informal and personal and are therefore normally reserved for persons with whom you have a fairly close relationship. "Sincerely," "Sincerely yours," and "Most sincerely," are friendly but a little less personal and are thus considered more appropriate for use with persons who are either unknown or unfamiliar to you.

A survey of several hundred cover letters recently received by our executive search firm revealed the following breakdown of usage of various types of complimentary closings:

| Complimentary Closing | Percent Usage |
| --- | --- |
| Sincerely, | 64% |
| Sincerely yours, | 20% |
| Very truly yours, | 14% |
| Yours very truly, | 2% |

It should be pointed out that these were cover letters addressed to various members of our staff, to whom the writers were either unknown or unfamiliar. This seems to suggest that, where you are unfamiliar with the addressee, it is safe to use any of the first three complimentary closings shown on the preceding chart. If you are on fairly personal terms with the addressee, however, it is recommended that you use a more appropriate closing, such as "Yours," "Regards," "Best regards," "Best wishes," and so forth. Such closings are more in keeping with a friendly relationship.

You will note that the complimentary closing is always followed by a comma. You will also note that it is only the initial word whose first letter is capitalized. The rest are all in lower case.

### Signature Line

The signature line is always positioned flush with the complimentary closing and at least four lines below it. This allows sufficient space for the author's signature. The exact positioning on the page depends upon the format of cover letter chosen, and is further explained later in the chapter.

The signature line contains the full formal name of the writer, including first name, middle initial (followed by a period), and surname. Although this may first appear overly formal in some cases, it should be remembered that the actual signature of the writer can be used to soften the tone of the signature line. Thus, if the author's formal name is Thomas J. Sanders, he might simply sign the letter "Tom" if that is in keeping with the nature of his relationship to the addressee.

Where the addressee is either unknown or unfamiliar to the author, it is recommended that the author sign his or her full formal name. Simply the first name or a nickname in such cases is considered inappropriate to the nature of the relationship.

### Typist Identification

The initials of the person typing the letter are always shown flush with the left margin, two lines below the signature block. These initials are typed in lower case. Thus, if the typist's name is George B. Smith, the letters "gbs" would appear on the left margin.

In those cases where you have dictated the cover letter, but your secretary or administrative assistant has typed and signed it, the identification line would consist of your initials (in capital letters), followed by a colon and then the initials of the typist (in lower case). If your name is Samuel B. Higgins and your secretary's name is Linda D. Britting, the identification line would read "SBH:ldb."

### Enclosure Line

Since your cover letter will normally include a résumé as a separate enclosure, this fact should be noted on the enclosure line, which is positioned flush with the typist identification and two lines immediately below.

If there is only a single enclosure, such as your résumé, the word "Enclosure" will suffice. If there are multiple documents enclosed (five, for example), this can be designated by "Enclosures (5)" or simply "Enclosures."

## Letter Formats

As stated earlier in this chapter, there are, essentially, only two acceptable formats to be used with the cover letter. These are the full block and the block/modified block. Since the modified block represents only a very slight alteration of the block format, for purposes of our discussion, I will treat these two formats as one.

Let's now examine these formats.

### *The Full Block Format*

The full block format is represented by Fig 2.1. As mentioned earlier, it is fairly popular and, according to my survey, it was used in 49 percent of several hundred cover letters received by our executive search firm.

Figure 2.1 reveals the distinguishing characteristics of the full block format when contrasted with the block/modified block style. Note that all components of the full block format—the return address, date, address, salutation, complimentary closing, signature line, typist identification, and enclosure line—are completely flush with the left margin of the letter.

From a typing efficiency standpoint, this format is slightly preferred over the block/modified block style. Since all lines of the full block layout are flush with the left margin, there are no indentations, which saves key strokes and therefore cuts down on the time and cost of producing the letter. This is an important (but not overriding) consideration.

Another benefit of the full block format is its neat, crisp, and easy-to-read appearance. It looks very uniform, structured, formal, and businesslike. It suggests to the reader that the author is likewise a neat, organized, structured, and businesslike person.

Although the full block format will likely serve you very well in your job hunting campaign (and I would not hesitate to recommend its use), in my judgment, there may be some advantages to using the block/modified block format instead. Let's take a look at these advantages.

### *Block and Modified Block Formats*

As stated earlier in the chapter, the block and modified block letter formats are also very popular. In fact, according to my survey, these styles, when combined, account for an estimated 51 percent of all cover letters. This suggests that they are slightly more popular than the full block format.

Review of the block and modified block formats (See Figures 2.2 and 2.3) reveals that they are substantially similar. Both indent the return address and datelines so that the longest line of these components is flush with the right margin of the letter. The complimentary closing and signature lines are also indented. These latter two lines may be indented in one of the following ways:

1.  Flush with the right margin
2.  Five spaces to the right of the center of the page
3.  Centered on the page

Regardless of positioning, however, the first letters of both the complimentary closing and the signature line are in vertical alignment.

The only difference between the block and the modified block is that the modified block provides for indentation of paragraphs. The first line of each new paragraph is indented five spaces. In the block layout, the first line of each paragraph is positioned flush with the left margin.

The remaining components in these two formats (address, salutation, body, typist identification, and enclosure line) are positioned flush with the left margin and are essentially identical to the full block format.

Like the full block format, the block and modified block formats are neat, well-organized, and easily read. In my judgment, however, they have two clear advantages over the full block format.

First, they provide more space for text than does the full block, because of the positioning of the return address and date line in relation to the first line of the address. You will note in the block and the modified block that the first line of the address is on the very next line following the date. By contrast, the full block requires three spaces between the dateline and the first line of the address. Either the block or the modified block layout will thus save three lines and allow more text in the body of the letter.

The second advantage these two formats have over the full block design is their tone. The full block is a structured, businesslike layout,

**FIGURE 2.1** *Full Block Format*

```
XXXXXXXXXXXXXXX        (return address)
XXXXXXXXXXXXXXX
XXXXXXXXXXXXXXX        (date)


XXXXXXXXXXXXXXX        (address)
XXXXXXXXXXXXXXX
XXXXXXXXXXXXXXX
XXXXXXXXXXXXXXX
XXXXXXXXXXXXXXX



XXXXXXXXXXXXXXX        (salutation)

XXXXXXXXXXXXXXXXXXXXXXXXXXXXXXXXXXXXXXXXXXXXXXXXXXXXXXXXXXXXXXX
XXXXXXXXXXXXXXXXXXXXXXXXXXXXXXXXXXXXXXXXXXXXXXXXXXXXXXXXXXXXXXX
XXXXXXXXXXXXXXXXXXXXXXXXXXXXXXXXXXXXXXXXXXXXXXXXXXXXXXXXXXXXXXX
XXXXXXXXXXXXXXXXXXXXXXXXXXXXXXXXXXXXXXXXXXXXXXXXXXXXXXXXXXXXXXX

XXXXXXXXXXXXXXXXXXXXXXXXXXXXXXXXXXXXXXXXXXXXXXXXXXXXXXXXXXXXXXX
XXXXXXXXXXXXXXXXXXXXXXXXXXXXXXXXXXXXXXXXXXXXXXXXXXXXXXXXXXXXXXX
XXXXXXXXXXXXXXXXXXXXXXXXXXXXXXXXXXXXXXXXXXXXXXXXXXXXXXXXXXXXXXX
XXXXXXXXXXXXXXXXXXXXXXXXXXXXXXXXXXXXXXXXXXXXXXXXXXXXXXXXXXXXXXX
XXXXXXXXXXXXXXXXXXXXXXXXXXXXXXXXXXXXXXXXXXXXXXXXXXXXXXXXXXXXXXX

XXXXXXXXXXXXXXXXXXXXXXXXXXXXXXXXXXXXXXXXXXXXXXXXXXXXXXXXXXXXXXX
XXXXXXXXXXXXXXXXXXXXXXXXXXXXXXXXXXXXXXXXXXXXXXXXXXXXXXXXXXXXXXX
XXXXXXXXXXXXXXXXXXXXXXXXXXXXXXXXXXXXXXXXXXXXXXXXXXXXXXXXXXXXXXX

XXXXXXXXXXXXXXXXXXXXXXXXXXXXXXXXXXXXXXXXXXXXXXXXXXXXXXXXXXXXXXX
XXXXXXXXXXXXXXXXXXXXXXXXXXXXXXXXXXXXXXXXXXXXXXXXXXXXXXXXXXXXXXX
XXXXXXXXXXXXXXXXXXXXXXXXXXXXXXXXXXXXXXXXXXXXXXXXXXXXXXXXXXXXXXX
XXXXXXXXXXXXXXXXXXXXXXXXXXXXXXXXXXXXXXXXXXXXXXXXXXXXXXXXXXXXXXX

XXXXXXXXXXXXXXX        (complimentary closing)


XXXXXXXXXXXXXXX        (signature line)

XXX                    (typist identification)

XXXXXXXXX              (enclosure line)
```

## FIGURE 2.2 *Block Format*

```
                         (return address)    XXXXXXXXXXXXXXX
                                             XXXXXXXXXXXXXXX
                                  (date)     XXXXXXXXXXXXXXX
XXXXXXXXXXXXXXX          (address)
XXXXXXXXXXXXXXX
XXXXXXXXXXXXXXX
XXXXXXXXXXXXXXX
XXXXXXXXXXXXXXX


XXXXXXXXXXXXXXX          (salutation)

XXXXXXXXXXXXXXXXXXXXXXXXXXXXXXXXXXXXXXXXXXXXXXXXXXXXXXXXXXXXXXXXXX
XXXXXXXXXXXXXXXXXXXXXXXXXXXXXXXXXXXXXXXXXXXXXXXXXXXXXXXXXXXXXXXXXX
XXXXXXXXXXXXXXXXXXXXXXXXXXXXXXXXXXXXXXXXXXXXXXXXXXXXXXXXXXXXXXXXXX
XXXXXXXXXXXXXXXXXXXXXXXXXXXXXXXXXXXXXXXXXXXXXXXXXXXXXXXXXXXXXXXXXX

XXXXXXXXXXXXXXXXXXXXXXXXXXXXXXXXXXXXXXXXXXXXXXXXXXXXXXXXXXXXXXXXXX
XXXXXXXXXXXXXXXXXXXXXXXXXXXXXXXXXXXXXXXXXXXXXXXXXXXXXXXXXXXXXXXXXX
XXXXXXXXXXXXXXXXXXXXXXXXXXXXXXXXXXXXXXXXXXXXXXXXXXXXXXXXXXXXXXXXXX
XXXXXXXXXXXXXXXXXXXXXXXXXXXXXXXXXXXXXXXXXXXXXXXXXXXXXXXXXXXXXXXXXX
XXXXXXXXXXXXXXXXXXXXXXXXXXXXXXXXXXXXXXXXXXXXXXXXXXXXXXXXXXXXXXXXXX

XXXXXXXXXXXXXXXXXXXXXXXXXXXXXXXXXXXXXXXXXXXXXXXXXXXXXXXXXXXXXXXXXX
XXXXXXXXXXXXXXXXXXXXXXXXXXXXXXXXXXXXXXXXXXXXXXXXXXXXXXXXXXXXXXXXXX
XXXXXXXXXXXXXXXXXXXXXXXXXXXXXXXXXXXXXXXXXXXXXXXXXXXXXXXXXXXXXXXXXX

XXXXXXXXXXXXXXXXXXXXXXXXXXXXXXXXXXXXXXXXXXXXXXXXXXXXXXXXXXXXXXXXXX
XXXXXXXXXXXXXXXXXXXXXXXXXXXXXXXXXXXXXXXXXXXXXXXXXXXXXXXXXXXXXXXXXX
XXXXXXXXXXXXXXXXXXXXXXXXXXXXXXXXXXXXXXXXXXXXXXXXXXXXXXXXXXXXXXXXXX
XXXXXXXXXXXXXXXXXXXXXXXXXXXXXXXXXXXXXXXXXXXXXXXXXXXXXXXXXXXXXXXXXX

                  (complimentary closing)    XXXXXXXXXXXXXXX


                         (signature line)    XXXXXXXXXXXXXXX

XXX             (typist identification)

XXXXXXXXX        (enclosure line)
```

FIGURE 2.3 *Modified Block Format*

```
                        (return address)   XXXXXXXXXXXXXXX
                                           XXXXXXXXXXXXXXX
                                (date)     XXXXXXXXXXXXXXX
XXXXXXXXXXXXXXX         (address)
XXXXXXXXXXXXXXX
XXXXXXXXXXXXXXX
XXXXXXXXXXXXXXX
XXXXXXXXXXXXXXX


XXXXXXXXXXXXXXX         (salutation)

    XXXXXXXXXXXXXXXXXXXXXXXXXXXXXXXXXXXXXXXXXXXXXXXXXXXXXXXXXX
XXXXXXXXXXXXXXXXXXXXXXXXXXXXXXXXXXXXXXXXXXXXXXXXXXXXXXXXXXXXXXX
XXXXXXXXXXXXXXXXXXXXXXXXXXXXXXXXXXXXXXXXXXXXXXXXXXXXXXXXXXXXXXX
XXXXXXXXXXXXXXXXXXXXXXXXXXXXXXXXXXXXXXXXXXXXXXXXXXXXXXXXXXXXXXX

    XXXXXXXXXXXXXXXXXXXXXXXXXXXXXXXXXXXXXXXXXXXXXXXXXXXXXXXXXX
XXXXXXXXXXXXXXXXXXXXXXXXXXXXXXXXXXXXXXXXXXXXXXXXXXXXXXXXXXXXXXX
XXXXXXXXXXXXXXXXXXXXXXXXXXXXXXXXXXXXXXXXXXXXXXXXXXXXXXXXXXXXXXX
XXXXXXXXXXXXXXXXXXXXXXXXXXXXXXXXXXXXXXXXXXXXXXXXXXXXXXXXXXXXXXX
XXXXXXXXXXXXXXXXXXXXXXXXXXXXXXXXXXXXXXXXXXXXXXXXXXXXXXXXXXXXXXX

    XXXXXXXXXXXXXXXXXXXXXXXXXXXXXXXXXXXXXXXXXXXXXXXXXXXXXXXXXX
XXXXXXXXXXXXXXXXXXXXXXXXXXXXXXXXXXXXXXXXXXXXXXXXXXXXXXXXXXXXXXX
XXXXXXXXXXXXXXXXXXXXXXXXXXXXXXXXXXXXXXXXXXXXXXXXXXXXXXXXXXXXXXX

    XXXXXXXXXXXXXXXXXXXXXXXXXXXXXXXXXXXXXXXXXXXXXXXXXXXXXXXXXX
XXXXXXXXXXXXXXXXXXXXXXXXXXXXXXXXXXXXXXXXXXXXXXXXXXXXXXXXXXXXXXX
XXXXXXXXXXXXXXXXXXXXXXXXXXXXXXXXXXXXXXXXXXXXXXXXXXXXXXXXXXXXXXX
XXXXXXXXXXXXXXXXXXXXXXXXXXXXXXXXXXXXXXXXXXXXXXXXXXXXXXXXXXXXXXX

                        (complimentary closing)   XXXXXXXXXXXXXXX


                             (signature line)   XXXXXXXXXXXXXXX
XXX             (typist identification)

XXXXXXXXX       (enclosure line)
```

which, to me, suggests a more formal, impersonal tone. This is the tone that you might expect when writing business to business.

By contrast, however, the other formats resemble that most widely used in personal correspondence. More specifically, the indentation used in both the block and modified block designs is similar to that in a personal letter and suggests a less formal, more personal tone that, in my judgment, is more in keeping with the tone you hope to create with the cover letter.

Although either the block or modified block style is perfectly acceptable for the cover letter, if given the choice, my selection would be the block format for the following reasons.

The cover letter is neither "business-to-business" nor "person-to-person" (personal) correspondence. Instead, it is "person-to-business." Thus, the format chosen should most closely match this "in-between" relationship.

As stated earlier, the full block format is the most formal, suggestive of business-to-business correspondence. On the other hand, the modified block format is identical to that used in most personal correspondence and may be slightly too personal in tone. By contrast, the block format (with its blocked paragraphs and indented return address, date, complimentary closing, and signature lines) is a cross between the full block and the modified block formats. Therefore, it seems to me most appropriate to the nature of the relationship and the "person-to-business" tone that the cover letter should convey.

In keeping with this logic, if you are well acquainted with the person to whom you are writing, by all means use the modified block format. In this case, both the full block and the block layouts are less appropriate, and the modified block format will better serve your purpose.

Enough said on the subject of cover letter format. Now let's move on to the actual cover letter itself. What should go into the body of the letter? What are the important points that need to be covered? How do you write an interesting cover letter that effectively markets your qualifications and motivates an employer to set up a job interview? These are the important subjects that will be answered in the ensuing chapters.

The next two chapters will deal with the important differences between good (effective) and poor (ineffective) cover letters. In each case, the elements and characteristics of good and poor cover letters are fully explained. To further make the point, actual samples of both are provided for your review and close examination.

# 3

# CHARACTERISTICS OF GOOD COVER LETTERS

In this chapter, we will be discussing good cover letters and their characteristics. What makes one cover letter effective and another drab and ineffective? Perhaps the best way to meaningfully address this question is to discuss the elements and characteristics of good and bad cover letters, and show some examples, so that you can actually see the differences. The focus of this chapter will be on good cover letters; the focus of the next chapter will be on those that are poorly written and ineffective.

Before getting started with our discussion, I strongly encourage you to spend a few moments carefully reviewing the four examples of good cover letters at the end of this chapter. You will find this review particularly helpful in understanding the points I will be making.

## Important Elements

Close examination of the sample cover letters provided at the end of this chapter will reveal that they exhibit certain similarities. These important similarities are:

1. An introductory paragraph that:

   a. is "interest generating,"
   b. states or implies employment interest.

2. A "value-selling" paragraph that:

   a. demonstrates your ability to be value adding,
   b. highlights your key strengths and abilities.

3. A "background summary" paragraph that briefly summarizes your relevant education and experience.

4. A statement that either "compels or ensures follow-up action."

5. A "statement of appreciation."

We will now proceed with a detailed discussion of each of these key elements for a fuller understanding of their importance to the success of an effective cover letter.

### *Introductory Paragraph*

The introductory paragraph is extremely key to the effectiveness of the employment cover letter. Essentially, it has two important objectives.

The first is to grab the reader's attention and thus compel the reader to continue reading the letter. The second is to establish your interest in employment (the purpose of the letter).

The first paragraph can render the cover letter useless if it fails to compel sufficient interest on the part of the reader to warrant his/her further reading. It is important, therefore, to get the reader's attention right from the start by opening your letter in an interesting manner.

Usually, if the reader senses that yours is one of those "mass-mailed, broadcast variety" letters that has been sent to hundreds of other executives, there is little incentive to read it. On the other hand, if there is some indication of personal knowledge of or connection with the company and the letter seems tailored to that specific reader or his or her organization, the reader's interest is usually heightened immediately and the probability of readership increases greatly.

Generally, there are three effective techniques for creating a personal, customized touch in the introductory paragraph. These are:

1. Use of personal contact
2. Use of specific company knowledge
3. Use of a compliment

Each of these can be reasonably effective in adding just that right amount of personal touch. Let's examine some examples of these three techniques.

Of the three interest-generating techniques mentioned here, the most effective is the use of personal contact. Cover letter sample C at the end of this chapter provides a good illustration of effective use of this technique.

You will note in sample C that the author has mentioned the name of a company employee, David Jenson, in the very first sentence of the introductory paragraph. Although the author does not state this, the implication is that Jenson and he are personal friends or acquaintances. Because of the wording, there is no way for the letter's recipient, William Clemson, to know just how close this relationship is. Jenson could be a very close personal friend or simply a brief acquaintance.

In this situation, where there is no immediate way to confirm the nature of the relationship, the general tendency is for the reader to "play it safe" and assume that the relationship is a fairly close one. In such cases, the reader usually feels obliged to read the cover letter with far greater care than if the letter were sent by someone not having a personal connection with the organization.

The lesson here should be clear. If you have a personal connection with the company to which you are writing, by all means use it in the opening paragraph of your letter. It will all but guarantee that your letter will be read.

In those cases where you are particularly interested in working for a specific employer and know no employees whom you can reference in your introductory paragraph, try cultivating such a contact within the company. This can normally be done with a little research and some creative networking. Here are some ways you can accomplish this.

1. *Industry Association Networking*   Using an industry association membership roster, identify key persons who, by title, would appear to be employed by your target firm in positions that are closely related to your field. Call these individuals, introduce yourself, and engage in some conversation about the company (e.g., products, markets, competition, strategy, etc.). You are now in a position to quote these people on the basis of these conversations.

2. *Professional Association Networking*   Join one or two professional associations and search the association membership roster for members currently employed by your target company. As with industry association networking, call these individuals and engage them in conversation about the company (its products, markets, competitors, management philosophy, strategies, job opportunities, etc.). Here again, you have made a contact you can quote in the introductory sentence of your cover letter.

3. *Literature Search*   If you can't identify employees through either a trade or a professional association membership roster, try doing so through a literature search. Using the computer facilities of a local library, try searching periodicals for articles that reference your target company. Many times, such articles will quote company employees whom you can contact. Using the articles you've found as the basis for initial discussion with these employees, you can soon lead the discussion toward topics of more immediate concern to your job search.

As you can see, it is relatively easy (with a little imagination, some basic research, and a simple telephone call) to develop a valuable contact at a target firm. Once you have talked with an employee, it is also a relatively easy matter to discover some ways of using the information obtained as ammunition for the lead sentence of your cover letter.

Here are some ways you can effectively introduce this personal contact at the beginning of the cover letter:

*During recent discussions with Steve Temple, your Manager of Accounting, I became aware of your concern about the need to automate the Accounts Payable function. Perhaps I can be of help.*

*Sandy Slagle, your Director of Marketing, was telling me that you may be looking for a Manager of Public Affairs. I am interested in talking with you about this position.*

*I have recently learned from Jane Swanson, your Director of Total Quality, about the work that you are currently doing in research with experimental design. As a Senior Research Statistician at Exxon's Research Center, this is a subject with which I am intimately familiar.*

*I recently learned from John Brighton, your Manufacturing Manager, that you are looking for a Senior Industrial Engineer. On the basis of John's description of some of the challenges that this position will face, I would be very interested in discussing this position with you.*

As you can see from these examples, in each case, there is a specific employee mentioned in the very first sentence of the introductory paragraph. Because of this "personal contact" type of introduction, it will be very difficult for the reader not to read the cover letter. Most will feel obligated to read it in the event that, at some future point, the referenced employee inquires about the letter and/or the author's employment status.

If you are unable to identify an employee to reference, another technique to generate reader interest is to make use of specific company knowledge. As with the "personal contact" technique, this serves to personalize the letter and take it out of the mass-mailed, broadcast category.

Sample B at the end of this chapter is an example of a cover letter that employs specific company information in the first paragraph as an interest generator. Most employers are impressed by a letter that shows an applicant has taken time to research the company. This is in sharp contrast to the hundreds of mass-mailed letters received by the employer in which it is evident that the prospective candidate knows little or nothing about the company.

If it is evident in the cover letter that the applicant has taken the time to research the company and personalize his or her letter, most employers will reciprocate by investing some time in reading it. The fact that the letter's author was sufficiently interested in employment with the company to do some research usually elicits very positive feelings on the part of the employer and serves to create a sense of obligation to read the cover letter with greater care and attention than that given to the mass-mailed, impersonal variety.

Sample B demonstrates effective use of this technique by a college student applying for a position as an accounting trainee. Notice how the student not only references the firm's college recruiting literature, but also uses the opening paragraph to relate this literature to her own job interests. In most cases, this sort of introduction will generate interest and compel the employer to read the rest of the cover letter.

Likewise, sample C makes use not only of personal contact but also of specific company knowledge. In this letter, Carla Davidson advises William Clemson, President of Carlton Chemicals, that she has learned that the company is seriously considering implementation of a Deming-based "total quality" program and may be in the market for someone to lead this effort. Clemson is likely to be somewhat surprised by and impressed with Carla's knowledge of his plans. As a result, he is highly likely to read all of Davidson's cover letter.

Here are some additional examples of introductory paragraphs that employ specific company knowledge to generate reader interest:

*I read the article concerning Champion Corporation's use of modern organization development techniques in the August 2 issue of* Business Week. *As a seasoned O.D. professional, I found this article unusually interesting, and it has prompted my decision to apply for employment with your company.*

*The recent article in the* TAPPI Journal *concerning Phillips Paper's decision to undertake a $1.2 billion capital expansion of its Mobile paper mill suggests that you may be in the market for experienced paper machine project engineers. If this is the case, you are likely to have an interest in my background.*

*Some recent research that I have done on your company reveals that in the last three years Cooper Technologies has taken the leadership in*

*the field of asbestos abatement. The fact that your sales have gone from
$8.2 million to over $40 million during this same period is most impressive. I would like to be affiliated with your company.*

*I recently read several articles concerning Dansforth Corporation's re-
search advances in the field of transparent electrophotography. The
electro-scanning technology used in this process is truly revolutionary
and exciting. I feel that my work as a photo-imaging scientist closely
parallels your research and that, as a result, you may have some interest
in my qualifications for employment with your company.*

As you can see, each of these introductory paragraphs makes very effective use of the specific company knowledge technique. There is a
very specific reference to some aspect of the company (e.g. growth,
products, technology, etc.) that makes it quite evident that the applicant
has taken the time to acquire some first-hand knowledge of the company. This conveys a level of personal interest the employer sees infre-
quently and serves to set you apart from the everyday job seeker who
applies to the company using an impersonal, mass-mailed broadcast
letter. The net result is to generate a heightened interest on the part
of the letter's recipient that is usually sufficient to warrant full reading
of the cover letter.

As mentioned earlier, another technique that can prove effective in
generating reader interest in your cover letter is using a compliment
in the introductory paragraph. Most employees have some pride in the
company for which they work. A complimentary remark normally ap-
peals to this sense of pride and thus creates interest in your cover letter.
The warm feelings you have created may well carry the reader through
the rest of your cover letter and reflect positively on your candidacy.

One caution about the use of the compliment technique! If you elect
to use a compliment, make sure that it is genuine and truly reflects
your feeling about the company. Nothing turns an employer off more
quickly than an insincere compliment. Such insincerity is normally
easily spotted and can cause the employer to feel that you are shallow
and insincere as well.

Most employers are insulted by insincere flattery. They feel that it is
an insult to their intelligence for the writer to think that he or she
could employ such a sham and expect to get away with it. The best rule
to follow here is, if you don't believe the compliment, don't use it.

In the executive search profession, we often receive cover letters that
use insincere flattery. It appears that certain outplacement or career

consulting firms are counseling job seekers to employ the complimentary technique in their cover letters to executive search consulting firms. Some examples of wording frequently employed by the clients of these firms are:

*An acquaintance of mine, whose judgment I respect, has highly recommended your firm as one of the outstanding executive search firms.*

*A colleague of mine has told me of your excellent reputation as an executive search firm that specializes in the recruitment of financial executives.*

*I recently learned about the reputation of The Bradford Group in the real estate industry. Several associates have told me about the high quality and reliability of your work in real estate search.*

*A colleague, whose opinion I respect, mentioned your quality search work in sales and marketing.*

Although, on the surface, these complimentary openings may seem both innocent and genuine, they are not. The problem is that I have received hundreds of cover letters using almost the exact same wording. Additionally, since we are a generalist firm that does not focus on or specialize in a particular area, it is quite obvious that people using these "canned" introductions have no direct knowledge of our firm. Thus, these introductions ring with insincerity and do little to increase my desire to read further.

The key word, then, in the use of the complimentary cover letter introduction is "sincerity." If you use a compliment, make sure it comes across as genuine and sincere.

Sample cover letter D uses the complimentary introduction. It compliments Mr. Harrison as someone who is "aware of the importance and value of a top flight Chief Financial Officer." Naturally, Mr. Harrison would like to think of himself as having this kind of awareness; so the compliment serves to hook his ego and will likely generate sufficient interest to motivate him to read on.

Some other examples of how the complimentary introduction might be used to generate reader interest follow:

*Because of the Shallinsworth Company's fine reputation as a market leader in the field of microwave electronics and its excellent reputation as an employer concerned with the development of its employees, I am interested in pursuing the possibility of employment. Accordingly, I am enclosing my resume for your review and consideration.*

*During my last five years as Sales Representative in the industrial fastener industry, I have watched Wilco Corporation's market entry and rapid rise to its current position as industry leader. Needless to say, your company's growth has been quite impressive. I would like to be a part of this growth and feel that I can further strengthen your market presence in the Southwest. Enclosed, therefore, please find my resume for your consideration.*

*Ever since I entered the field of pharmaceutical research in 1982, I have admired the quality of Benson Laboratory's work in the field of cardiovascular research. As a research scientist with over twenty patents and a reputation for creativity in the same field, I would appreciate the opportunity to explore the possibility of a position as a member of your respected research staff.*

*I recently read your article on Barnsworth Company's commitment to the participatory management concept, and I was quite impressed. I have long been an advocate of the participatory management concept and firmly believe that it is the only way to unleash and capitalize on an organization's full human resource potential.*

*Your comments have piqued my interest, and I would therefore appreciate the opportunity to discuss how I might assist Barnsworth to further capitalize on this exciting concept as an internal O.D. consultant to the company.*

*I have long admired The Wadsworth Company's excellent reputation as a market leader in the field of specialty chemicals. Mr. Baskerville, as the Director of Market Research for a company that enjoys such market preeminence, you must, I am sure, derive a great deal of professional satisfaction from your work and the contributions you have made to your employer as its marketing leader. I am fascinated with the idea of being part of a marketing research organization such as yours, and would welcome the opportunity to explore this possibility during a personal interview.*

As you can see, using the complimentary introductory paragraph can be quite effective in generating reader interest in your cover letter and résumé. The personal nature of these complimentary remarks, in most cases, will ensure that your letter is read by the employer, increasing the possibility of a subsequent interview.

Again, of the three interest-generating techniques described here, the most effective is the use of personal contacts. Both specific company knowledge and the complimentary introduction, however, can also serve your purpose rather nicely. All three are a substantial improvement over the typical introductory remarks found in most mass-mailed cover letters, and can provide you with the competitive edge you will need to get the employer's attention and increase the possibility of landing that all-important interview.

## Value-Selling Paragraph

Another key characteristic of effective cover letters is the use of the "value-selling" paragraph. This is the paragraph that describes the value you can bring to the hiring organization and that provides the basis for motivating the employer to invite you for an interview.

A well-written value-selling paragraph is not simply a sterile listing of your strengths. Instead, it lists specific results achieved and contributions made in other firms and states or implies that you can make similar contributions to the prospective employer's firm as well. The inference that will normally be drawn by the prospective employer is that you are someone who is capable of adding value to his or her organization. You already have a track record that demonstrates this.

Modern interview theory subscribes to the principle that the best predictor of future performance is past performance in the same or similar areas. This is the basis for behavior-based interviewing. Employers are looking for tangible evidence of the ability to do certain things. Thus, the candidate's capabilities and qualifications are normally judged by specific results achieved in certain key areas thought to be critical or important to good job performance.

The purpose of the value-selling paragraph, therefore, is to facilitate the employer's evaluation process. By citing results achieved in areas thought to be critical to good job performance, you are providing tangible evidence of your ability to perform in these important areas and, thereby, to add value to the organization.

Usually, the dilemma faced at this juncture by most cover letter authors is deciding which specific results to highlight. Which ones will be truly value adding from the employer's perspective? Unfortunately, many job seekers ignore that question and choose to highlight those contributions of which they are most proud, with little regard to the probable needs of the employer. This is a serious mistake!

If you are tempted to do this, you need to go back to basics. One of the fundamental mistakes made by most salespersons is to begin lauding attributes of the product or service he or she is selling without first understanding the specific needs of the customer. Hence, the salesperson will drone on and on, covering information that is of little or no real interest to the customer. The end result is loss of the sale.

Successful salespersons, on the other hand, have always known that the sale must be focused on customer needs. What motivates one customer to buy may not motivate another. One may be looking for price; another, quality; another, ease of operation; another, time savings; another, cost savings; another, aesthetics; and so on. Not determining and qualifying these needs in advance may result in emphasizing product attributes that are not important to a particular customer. Even worse, it may cause the salesperson to neglect key product attributes that would more than satisfy the customer's needs and result in a sale.

An analogy can be drawn with selling your attributes in the cover letter. If you are to create an image of yourself as someone who can be value adding and who can contribute in areas important to the employer, you must first start with an understanding of the employer's needs—those key areas where he or she is likely to be looking for improvement. When determining this, ask yourself these questions:

1. What key problems is the employer looking to solve?
2. What similar problems have you successfully solved? What were the results?
3. What is the organization's future strategy?
4. What changes will it need to drive to achieve these strategic goals?
5. What new problems will need to be solved to bring these changes about?
6. What similar problems have you successfully solved? With what results?
7. What new methods or technology is the employer attempting to apply? For what purpose?
8. How have you applied such methods or technology? With what results?

Ideally, to write a highly effective value-selling paragraph, you should use your networking contacts within the target company to research these questions in advance of designing your cover letter and résumé.

The answers will allow you to tailor these documents to the specific needs of the employer, thus stacking the deck in your favor and substantially increasing your chances of a successful outcome. I would strongly recommend that you do this for the dozen or so target companies for which you would most like to work. It will have substantial payoff!

In cases where the remaining number of target firms is simply too large to warrant individual research, I suggest that you sort them into industry groupings and then conduct some good industry research. Some important questions to keep in mind when performing such research are:

1. What are the major problems confronting this industry?
2. What knowledge and skills are required to solve problems?
3. What are the major trends and changes being pursued by companies within this industry?
4. What new knowledge (e.g., methods, technology, techniques, etc.) is required to facilitate these changes?
5. What specific knowledge, skills, and capabilities do you possess that will enable you to:
   a. solve these major industry problems,
   b. drive these desired changes or trends?
6. What evidence can you cite of your overall capabilities in these important areas (i.e., results achieved, contributions made, etc.)?

By answering these and similar questions, you will automatically develop the ammunition for writing a good value-selling paragraph that is focused on the key needs of the industry. These needs, of course, will reflect the individual needs of many of the organizations in each industry grouping. You are once again stacking the deck in your favor by appealing to the specific needs of most of these member companies. This should serve to substantially increase the odds for a favorable result.

The four sample cover letters at the end of this chapter provide examples of value-selling paragraphs. Each paragraph, as you will see, focuses on the ability of the author to contribute something of value to the employer. Note that it is not simply a delineation of the candidate's strengths; each paragraph focuses on his or her ability to make specific contributions that will in some way prove beneficial to the hiring organization.

The value-selling paragraph provides a key opportunity to market yourself to prospective employers and to motivate them to act favorably on your employment candidacy. If carefully thought out and well-written, this paragraph can make a significant difference in the effectiveness of your cover letter and result in many more interview opportunities. It must be well-written, however, and, to maximize effectiveness, must be focused on the real needs of the employer. Perhaps no other paragraph is more important to cover letter effectiveness.

### Background Summary

In reviewing the sample cover letters at the end of this chapter, you will note that another characteristic they exhibit in common is use of the background summary. The background summary provides a brief synopsis of your relevant education and experience. Usually, it includes the academic degree held, major field of study, number of years of experience, and a short description of job-relevant experience.

The purpose of this summary is to convey to the employer that you have the appropriate training, experience, and seasoning to support the position for which you are applying. Keep this summary brief, since it is intended to be only a short synopsis of relevant education and experience and is not intended to replace the full résumé that accompanies the cover letter.

### Action Statement

Any expert in the field of advertising and promotion will tell you that for a sales letter to be effective, it should contain an action statement that somehow ensures action beyond simply reading the letter. Your cover letters should include a statement that urges the employer to take favorable action on your employment candidacy or that tells the employer that you intend to take action by calling to determine interest and, if appropriate, arrange for an interview.

Examples of action statements from the sample letters at the end of the chapter are shown below.

*I will plan to call you next week to determine if you are interested in discussing this matter further and, if appropriate, to arrange for a meeting with you.*

*I would appreciate the opportunity to discuss how I might further contribute to the Dixon Company's research efforts through a personal interview. I will call you on Tuesday, March 28, to determine your interest and, if appropriate, to arrange for a personal meeting.*

*I would be pleased to have the opportunity to interview with your college recruiting representative during your January recruiting schedule, and hope that you will give the enclosed résumé favorable consideration.*

*Should you be in the market for a top flight financial officer who can add profits to your bottom line, I would appreciate hearing from you.*

Here are some additional examples of action statements for your consideration.

*I will plan to call you on the afternoon of September 30 to determine your interest and, if agreeable, to arrange for a personal meeting.*

*I will call your office on Wednesday, January 15, to determine your interest and a suitable time for a meeting with your recruiter.*

*Should you have an appropriate opening in your Research Center, I would welcome the opportunity to meet with you personally. I can be reached at (315) 455-7224 during the day and (315) 467-9951 during evenings and weekends. I look forward to hearing from you.*

Although this may prove too time consuming and impractical if you are currently employed, wherever possible, you should take the initiative by offering to call the prospective employer. In this way, there is nothing left to chance. Besides politely forcing the employer to take action on your candidacy, this technique has the advantage of providing you with a contact for further networking, even if the employer has no further interest in your candidacy.

## Statement of Appreciation

The final hallmark of a good cover letter is courtesy. Since most employers are very busy people, you should express your appreciation for the time they are taking to review and consider your employment credentials. A simple statement of appreciation will suffice.

The following are some examples of statements of appreciation:

*Thank you for your consideration.*

*I appreciate your consideration of my credentials, and look forward to hearing from you.*

*I hope that you will give the enclosed résumé favorable consideration. Thank you.*

*Thank you for your consideration. I look forward to hearing from you shortly.*

Although one or more of the elements discussed in this chapter may be missing from a given letter, my experience has convinced me that these are the basic characteristics contained in most effective cover letters. Letters that are well designed for maximum effectiveness, in my judgment, should thus attempt to incorporate all of them.

135 Elm Street
Adrian, MI 18736
March 12, 1991

Mr. William Fowler
Vice of Research
The Dixon Company
Suite 216
199 Commerce Way
Detroit, MI 19285

Dear Mr. Fowler:

*Statement of Interest*

With this letter, I wish to express my strong interest in seeking employment with The Dixon Company as a Senior Statistician in your research center. Accordingly, a complete resume is enclosed for your review and consideration.

*Value Selling*

Of probable interest to you is the fact that I can substantially improve the overall efficiency and effectiveness of your research efforts through the application of various statistical methodologies. By training your staff in design of experiments, laboratory experiments can be conducted with much greater accuracy and predictability. Through consulting support in such areas as variance analysis, I can also help your staff to identify, isolate, study and understand those variables critical to process performance and product quality.

*Background Summary*

I hold a Ph.D. in Applied Statistics, have over 15 years research experience, and am thoroughly versed in a wide range of statistical methods, including: design of experiments, variance analysis, regression analysis, process capability studies, statistical process control, etc.

*Compelling Action*

I would appreciate the opportunity to discuss how I might further contribute to The Dixon Company's research efforts though a personal interview. I will call you on Tuesday, March 28, to determine your interest and, if appropriate, to arrange for a personal meeting.

*Statement of Appreciation*

Thank you for your consideration.

Sincerely,

*Judith A. Parker*

Judith A Parker

jap

Enclosure

## SAMPLE B *Good Cover Letter*

206 Lancart Street
Arlington, VA 18496
November 16, 1993

Ms Carolyn A. Beatty
Manager of Corporate Accounting
Central Electric Company
825 River View Road
Utica, NY 84726

Dear Ms Beatty:

*Use of Company Knowledge + Statement of Interest*

Review of your company's college recruiting literature indicates that you hire Accounting Trainees as entry-level employees in the Corporate Accounting function. The idea of having rotational assignments in auditing, tax compliance and cost accounting sounds extremely interesting to me, and I am therefore interested in interviewing with your firm during your forthcoming recruiting trip to George Washington University.

*Value Selling*

I will be receiving a B.S. degree in Accounting in June of next year. I have been a strong student and have been recognized by the university for my academic achievement through receipt of various awards and scholarships, which are detailed on my enclosed resume.

*Value Selling*

In addition to my academic achievement, you will note that I have always been industrious and hard working. This is evidenced by the fact that I have been continually employed, either full or part-time, since age thirteen. Despite this, I have always managed to squeeze in a fair number of extracurricular activities, which, I hope, demonstrates my ability to effectively organize and plan my time to maximum advantage.

*Value Selling*

My solid academic performance, work ethic, drive, organization skills, and strong interest in the accounting field will, I hope, convince you that I have the basic ingredients to make a valuable addition to Central Electric's Accounting function.

*Statement of Appreciation*

I would be pleased to have the opportunity to interview with your college recruiting representative during your January recruiting schedule, and hope that you will give the enclosed resume favorable consideration. Thank you.

Sincerely,

*Margaret R. Temple*

Margaret R. Temple
Student

mrt

Enclosure

126 Duabert Street
Reading, PA 19475
March 12, 1991

Mr. William C. Clemson, President
Carlton Chemicals, Inc.
1825 East Market Street
Philadelphia, PA 19736

Dear Mr. Clemson:

*Use of Personal Contact*

During recent discussions with your Director of Manufacturing, David Jenson, I was advised that you are seriously considering the implementation of a Deming-based "total quality" program at Carlton Chemicals, and may be in the market for someone who can provide strong leadership to this effort. If you are seeking such leadership, you may well be interested in my credentials as a manager in the field of total quality.

*Background Summery*

A Ph.D. in Applied Statistics, I have over fifteen years experience in the field of quality and quality management. I have been thoroughly trained in Deming's management principles and am skilled in the application of such statistical methodology as experimental design, process capability studies, variance analysis, statistical process control, etc. I enjoy national recognition as a professional statistician and have been named a Fellow of the American Statistical Association.

*Value Selling*

More important, I have provided the strategic leadership to Cassach Chemical Company in the development and implementation of a highly successful, corporate-wide "total quality" effort, which has been credited with substantially improving the company's overall performance. In 1989, for example, the company realized a $10 million earnings improvement that was directly attributable to this program. I feel that similar contributions might be made to your firm as well.

*Compelling Action*

Perhaps we should plan to meet to explore how I might be able to assist you in realizing substantive results through the implementation of an effective total quality effort at Carlton Chemical. I will plan to call you next week to determine if you are interested in discussing this matter and, if appropriate, to arrange for a meeting with you.

I look forward to meeting you.

Sincerely,

Carla F. Davidson

Carla F. Davidson

CFD:anr

Enclosure

51

## SAMPLE D *Good Cover Letter*

718 Mockingbird Lane
Falls Church, VA 17395
July 23, 1992

Mr. Craig F. Harrison
President & Chief Operating Officer
Wellsboro Manufacturing Company
Lee & Green Streets
Boston, MA 35771

Dear Mr. Harrison:

*Use of Compliment*

As a top executive of a leading company in the electronics manufacturing field, you are aware, I am sure, of the importance and value of a top flight Chief Financial Officer. If you are in the market for such an individual, you may want to give serious consideration to my employment candidacy.

*Background Summary + Value Selling*

With over fifteen years of progressively senior financial management experience in electronics manufacturing, I have logged a very satisfying record in such important areas as cash flow improvement, profit enhancement and application of sophisticated MIS techniques. As Chief Financial Officer with my current employer, a $500 million manufacturer of integrated circuits, I have established an excellent reputation for effective cost control. Under my strategic leadership, cost reduction task forces have contributed a 25% improvement in net profits during the last two years alone.

*Reason for Job Search*

Since my current company is a family-owned enterprise, it has become clear to me that meaningful career growth is simply not a realistic probability. I have therefore decided to seek employment elsewhere.

*Compensation Requirements*

My current compensation is $95K per year plus bonus. My requirements are in the $100K range plus comprehensive benefits package.

*Compelling Action + Statement of Appreciation*

Should you be in the market for a top flight financial officer who can add profits to your bottom line, I would appreciate hearing from you.

Sincerely yours,

*Susan B. Fleming*

Susan B. Fleming

drs

Enclosure

# 4

# CHARACTERISTICS OF POOR COVER LETTERS

We learned in the preceding chapter that there are certain common characteristics of good cover letters. These characteristics are:

1. An "interest-generating" first paragraph that grabs the reader's interest.
2. A "value-selling" paragraph that focuses on employer needs and demonstrates the ability to solve key problems and drive strategic change.
3. A "background summary" paragraph that capsules relevant education and experience.
4. An "action-compelling" statement that either compels or ensures follow-up action.
5. A statement of appreciation.

### Elements of Bad Cover Letters

It should stand to reason that poor letters are generally characterized by the absence of one or more of these important elements. But, although this is certainly true, there are other factors that can account for the lack of impact and effectiveness. The focus of this chapter will be on these additional characteristics that contribute to overall cover letter ineffectiveness. They are:

1. Poor overall appearance
2. Poor grammar, punctuation and misspelled words
3. Rambling—lack of focus
4. Self-focused versus employer focused
5. Bland, boring text
6. Gross exaggeration—bragging
7. Aggressive, pushy tone
8. Self-deprecation

Let's examine each of these detracting characteristics in detail, so that you can more fully appreciate the effect they have on cover letter effectiveness. To facilitate this, I have included sample cover letters that exhibit them. The chapter is arranged so that a corresponding sample immediately follows discussion of each of these negative characteristics.

## *Poor Overall Appearance*

Sample A depicts a cover letter that has poor overall appearance.

Perhaps the most frequent crime of cover letter authors is to cram too much information onto the page. Sample A is a typical example of this. Note how the text is pushed out against the left and right margins of the letter, leaving almost no white space as a neat frame. This contributes to an overall sloppy appearance and detracts substantially from the letter's effectiveness.

Careful review of this sample also reveals that it does not fully conform to acceptable cover letter format, as discussed in Chapter 2. Although it generally follows the standard block format, its complimentary close and signature line should not be flush with the left hand margin, but should be positioned in line with the return address and date line at the top. Further, Mr. Stewart's title is missing, and there is no space provided between the salutation and the first line of the initial paragraph. In addition, the signature has been crammed against the bottom of the page so that there is no room to include a typed signature line immediately below Simpleton's signature.

This departure from acceptable format contributes to the letter's poor appearance, detracting from both the aesthetics and general balance of the letter's layout.

Failure to provide space between paragraphs causes the text to flow together and makes it somewhat difficult to read. Space between paragraphs would have set them apart and would have substantially improved both appearance and readability.

Also detracting from the overall appearance of this letter are the many misspelled words, typographical errors, and resultant manual corrections to the text. Although you would expect to see this kind of thing on a first or second draft, it should never appear on the final copy that is sent to an employer. All such changes should be made on the draft, and the final document should be flawless.

When a cover letter of this sort is received by a prospective employer, the impression created is a very poor one. It suggests that the candidate who has sent it is very disorganized and sloppy. Most employers will not even bother to read such a poorly prepared letter and will simply move on to the next candidate.

# SAMPLE A *Poor Cover Letter*
## *(Poor Overall Appearance)*

116 Lawrence Street
Winslow, ME 19774
June 5, 19905

Mr. David G. Stewart
The Greenboro Company
1836 Valentie Street
Greenboro, NY 18746

Dear Mr. Stewart:

I am writing to you to ask for a job.  I know there are a lot of good reasons for you to hire me, and I think that we should get together to discuss them.  I am really quite a good saleman.

I went to school at Brighton University and got a degree in Marketing. Then I went to work for the Hillsboro Company as a Salesman.  I worked there from 1969 to 1971.  I did a really good job at Hillsboro and got the Salesman of the Year award which was awarded to me by the President.  I almost doubled the sales during the 2 years I was there. But, I was unhappy with my compensation and decided to quit and go to work with  for the Merritt Tool Company in Jackson, Michigan.

While working for Merritt, I was the Regional Sales Manager for the Northeat Region and covered New Hampshire, Vermont, Massachusetts, Upstate New York and Maine. In 1973, the territory was enlarged to include Connecticut and Rhode Island.  I sold power tools to retail stores and contractors and did really well. I increased sales for my territory by 5% for every year I was at Merritt./ Finally, I got into an argument with my boss over territory boundaries and decided to quit.

I really didn't like the way I was treated at Merritt. My former boss always had a habit of bugging me about my daily call reports and constantly complained about their content. He didn,t do this to other Sales Representatives, so I felt that he was picking on me.  As a result, I quit without notice. Consequently, I will  probably not get a very good reference from Merritt Tools.  You need to know this in advance.

My background includes over 30 years selling power tools to retail and industrial accounts and contractors.  I managed groups of up to 32 salespersons and covered nearly the whole United States at on time or another.  I have also taken a number of sales courses and really know how to sell. I am also very aggressive and am not afraid to ask for the order.  I am also very good at managing other people.

I am a very high energy person, and I am extremely well motivated.  I like to travel a lot, and have sometimes traveled as much as 85% of the time.

Last year I earned $65,000. I also had a car and expenses as well as use of a country club membership.  I would need an increase of at least 25% if I am expected to move out of the Winslow area.  This is, of course, due to the cost of living.  The company that hires me will also have to agree to reimburse all moving expenses.  If possible, I would prefer not to relocate, however, since my family much prefers to remain in Maine.

I hope that you will cyall me soon, so that we can arrange for a job interview. I asure you, it will really be worth your time!  I can really do a lot for your company and help you to increase your sales volume quite a bit. We should definitely meet at your earliest convenience.

I can furnish excellent reference if you need them. Many of my customers will speak out in my behalf. The best reference for a salesman, as you know, is a satisfied customer.

Very respectfully yours,

*[signature]*

133 Warren Street
Springfield, OH 19485
March 26, 1992

Mr. George S. Rawlings
Director of Manufacturing
Spaaling, Inc.
625 West Oxnard Street
Toledo, OH 94852

Dear Mr. Rawlings:

I seen your newspaper advertisemant in the New Yoark Times for a
Managar of Manufacturing Services, working at you Lawndale Plant in
Lawndale Ohio. I am interested in this position very much and would
appreciete the opputunity to interview with you for this job. I
feal that you will be empressed with my excellent cradentials for
this position.

My bakground includes a B.S. degree in Business Administreation
plus more then seventean years experieance in manufacturing
management. Of particular interst should be the fact that I warked
for your competitor, Warrington Corporation, as ZManagar of
Manufacturing for nearly six years.

Some of my major ackomplishments include:

1. Decreased manufacturing costs by allmost 30 parcent thru
   instalation of new production skeduling system.

2. Started up nue steel boldt manufacturing line 3 weaks
   ahaead of skedule with compleetly trained crews.

3. Installed Just-In-Time inventory system that redused
   inventory capitol investment by more then 34%.

I know that I can make a reel contribution to your company and I
feel that you should give serous consideration to hiring me. Lets
us plan to get together and talk about the perspects of my
employment with yur company. I will plan to call you all next
Wensday to skedule a meeting to discuss our mutual interests.

Thank you for yar concideration.

Sincerely,

*Kevin G. Numbskull*

Kevin G. Numbskull

### Poor Grammar, Punctuation, and Misspelled Words

Sample B depicts a cover letter that is loaded with misspelled words and poor punctuation and grammar. Although the letter is neat and well designed, the reader's initial positive impressions of the candidate are, unfortunately, quickly dispelled once he or she begins to wade into the text.

Poor grammar, bad punctuation, and misspelled words suggest that the applicant is either poorly educated or simply doesn't care about the impression created. Obviously, if he is applying for a position that requires good verbal and written communication skills, the author of this letter, Mr. Numbskull, has done little to endear himself to the prospective employer. The chances are unusually high that the employer is going to forgo reading the accompanying résumé and quickly move on to the next job applicant.

Few things can turn an employer off more quickly than poor English. If you are not particularly adept in this area, I strongly suggest that you have a knowledgeable friend proofread your cover letter very thoroughly before going to press.

### Rambling—Lack of Focus

A nonfocused, rambling cover letter can suggest to a prospective employer that the author is verbose and poorly organized. Such a letter is represented by sample C.

You will note, in reviewing sample C, that a major contributing factor in its nonfocused, rambling style is the use of unnecessary words. As an exercise that should help you avoid writing this kind of a letter, try editing the sample letter, removing all words that do not add information or lend meaning. Next, try rewriting each sentence of the remaining text more concisely. Can you convey the same thoughts with fewer words? With a little effort, you'll be amazed at the results you get.

Although sample C contains a lot of information, this information is not presented in a meaningful, compelling way that motivates the employer to take action. It would appear to be simply a summary of the applicant's background that does little to focus on selling the employer on the value the author can add to the firm. It is a bland recital of the writer's education and employment history with a few random thoughts thrown in concerning personal traits and philosophy. And none of it is woven together particularly well.

# SAMPLE C *Poor Cover Letter*
## *(Rambling—Lack of Focus)*

200 East Shinning Lane
Sunnyville, CA 89375
July 2, 1990

Ms Katherine Jenkins
Director of Public Affairs
The Kingston Company
325 Westover Blvd.
Seattle, WA 19746

Dear Ms Jenkins:

I am very interested in employment with your company, and I am therefore submitting my resume for your review. I think you will find my background very interesting. Please consider my credentials for any available openings.

I hold a B.S. degree in Communications from Brightling University, where I excelled as a student. I earned the Koller's Award for contribution to my community and remain, to this day, very active in community service.

I am considered a very outgoing, friendly person by all those who know me. When asked to describe Ron, most would probably use such adjectives as open, honest, sincere, dedicated and hard working. I have always been very dedicated to my work and loyal to my employers. I am well motivated and am capable of carrying out my work with little or no supervision.

Following graduation from Brightling, I spent three years in the Peace Corps, where I learned the true meaning of life. I came to appreciate the importance of the small things of life and the value of personal relationships. These basic values have served me well in the business world, as I have pursued my career goals.

My background includes nearly twelve years in the field of Public Affairs. Most recently, I have been employed as Manager of Contributions for the Ballingar Company, a $3 billion manufacturer of consumer products. In this capacity, I have managed an annual contributions budget of $1.2 million. I have also spent nearly three years as Supervisor of Customer Inquiry, a position that I thoroughly enjoyed.

Thank you for your consideration, Ms Jenkins, and I look forward to hearing from you.

Sincerely,

*Ronald R. Rambling*

Ronald R. Rambling

rrr

Enclosure

Rambling letters will not promote your employment candidacy and can, in fact, negatively affect your efforts. Try to design letters that are concise and well focused in support of your stated job objective.

## Self-Focused Versus Employer-Focused

Sample D depicts a letter that is self- rather than employer-focused. There is little in this letter that will convince the employer of the candidate's ability to add value to the hiring organization.

This letter clearly focuses on the needs of the applicant. It describes the reason for her job search, the type of position sought, the organizational culture sought, and compensation requirements. She does nothing to address the needs of the employer.

Bear in mind that employers hire people because of their ability to add value to the organization. They are not interested in the applicant's demands but in his or her ability to solve key problems, help achieve strategic objectives, apply state-of-the-art methods, and so forth.

A self-focused cover letter that does not address your capability to make meaningful contributions to the firm falls considerably short of its primary purpose. It will do little to convince the employer that there are good reasons to interview you. Instead, it will create an impression that you are self-centered and concerned only with your own needs, and it will not help you win the all-important employment interview.

## Bland, Boring Text

Sample E is an example of a cover letter that employs bland and boring text. Unfortunately, it is all too typical of the cover letters received by employers and executive search firms.

Generally, this type of letter is characterized by a bland presentation of educational credentials and an unexciting summary of professional work experience. Moreover, there is no attempt to relate these credentials to the needs of the target organization. Such letters also tend to be verbose, containing a lot of unnecessary words that add little to the information already presented.

A bland, boring letter does not excite the prospective employer's imagination. It tends to suggest that the author lacks creativity and resourcefulness—the personal traits toward which an employer will gravitate when looking for persons who can bring fresh new ideas and solutions to the firm's drive to achieve competitive advantage in the

814 Bushnell Lane
Shady Grove, NY 89374
June 15, 1995

Mr. Carl C. Lukens
Vice President of Manufacturing
Walton Electronics, Inc.
126 Cursor Avenue
Bricktown, NY 18736

Dear Mr. Lukens:

A recent staff reduction at Burton Electronics has resulted in
the layoff of over 40% of the salaried staff. Unfortunately, my
position as Manufacturing Manager - Printed Circuits has been
eliminated, and I am now forced to seek employment elsewhere.

I am seeking a position in manufacturing management with a medium-
to large-sized electronics manufacturing company. I prefer
working for a company that has demonstrated significant growth in
recent years and whose prospects for continued growth appear
excellent. I also seek a position that offers defined opportunity
for future growth to the senior management level.

The company I seek will be a firm believer in the use of
participatory management principles. They will believe that the
proper role of a manager is to serve as a coach, teacher and
facilitator. Further, they will be committed to a strong belief
in the concept of management through others rather than the
management of things.

My compensation requirements are in the $80,000 range, with the
opportunity for review and increase on an annual basis. I will
also require a comprehensive benefits package.

To arrange for an employment interview, please call me at (212)
875-2864. I look forward to hearing from you shortly.

Sincerely,

*Barbara A. Mattson*

Barbara A. Mattson

bam

Enclosure

### SAMPLE E *Poor Cover Letter*
### *(Bland, Boring Text)*

122 Oyster Road
Kingston, RI 17364
May 23, 1992

Mr. Raymond D. Barker
Manager of Corporate Accounting
Blakesmith Company, Inc.
112 Freund Road
Lancaster, PA. 19746


Dear Mr. Barker:

I am writing to you for the purpose of applying for the position
of Cost Accountant with the Blakesmith Company, Inc. I have
enclosed a copy of my resume for your review. I trust that this
resume will contain all of the information that you will need to
make a proper evaluation of my employment candidacy; however, if
additional information is required, please advise me and I will
be pleased to furnish whatever you require.

As you can see from the enclosed employment resume, I earned a
B.S. degree in Accounting from Villanova University, where I
graduated in 1987. Following graduation from Villanova, my
professional career began with Price Waterhouse, where I worked
as an Auditor for four years. I resigned from Price Waterhouse in
1991, to accept employment as a Cost Accountant with Hornhaffle
Company. I have now worked at Hornhaffle for nearly seven years,
and I have recently decided to seek employment elsewhere.

I have been a good employee for my past employers. I have had
excellent attendance and have missed only four days of work in
eleven years. Additionally, my performance has always been rated
as satisfactory, and I can furnish good business and personal
references if this is required.

I am currently earning $42,000 per year with Hornhaffle, and my
next salary increase is due in July of this year. These increases
have normally run in the 8 to 10% range. My minimum salary
requirements with a new employer would therefore be in the high-
$40K range.

Please review the enclosed employment resume and let me know if
you have any appropriate openings. Thank you for your
consideration.

Respectfully yours,

*Blandon B. Bland*

Blandon B. Bland

erm

marketplace. Such a lack of imagination will not help you to stand out from the masses and will likely cause the prospective employer to move on to the next applicant.

Employment cover letters need to convey a certain sense of excitement and enthusiasm. They need to demonstrate that the author is alive, alert, resourceful, creative, and anxious to make a valuable contribution to his or her next employer. Bland, boring cover letters hardly accomplish this objective.

### Gross Exaggeration—Bragging

Another mistake frequently made by cover letter authors is to cross over the fine line between emphasizing strengths and outright bragging. Sample F crosses this line and thus reflects poorly on the author.

Generally, the most common cause of a letter's somewhat bragging tone is the overuse of superlatives, which tends to make the writer appear insincere and untruthful. The result is an aura of being "bigger than life," and the employer thus begins to question the applicant's credibility. There is also sometimes a very fine line between bragging and exaggeration, or lying.

Most employment experts would agree that it is important to "toot your own horn" in the employment process. You do need to emphasize your strengths, accomplishments, and attributes in a positive and energetic way. It is important, however, that you do so in a socially acceptable way and that you not lose credibility with your audience. If you fail to use good taste in tooting your own horn, your cover letter can be very damaging (or even fatal) to your employment campaign.

If you suspect that you may be coming across too strongly, have someone critique your letter for tone. Ask if it sounds as if you are bragging and request assistance in choosing words that will tone things down a bit but still help you to make your point.

### Aggressive, Pushy Tone

Tone is very important to the effectiveness of your cover letter. Although you want to be assertive and motivate the reader to take appropriate action, be careful that you don't come across as aggressive or pushy.

Sample G is an example of an aggressive, pushy letter. The tone of a letter crosses the fine line between assertiveness and aggressiveness when the language that is used becomes offensive to the reader. In

615 Bellingsway Road
Meadowville, TX 93827
January 15, 1997

Ms Wanda Maddrey-Randolph
Vice President of Sales & Marketing
Koehler Manufacturing Company
133 Printer's Place
Dansforth, MI 19386

Dear Ms Maddrey-Randolph:

As Vice President of Sales & Marketing for a well-known
manufacturing company, I'm sure that you recognize an outstanding
salesperson when you see one. I am sure, following review of my
enclosed resume, that you will agree that I am one of the best
sales professionals that you have ever seen! Why don't we plan to
get together and talk?

My record will show that I have consistently been one of the top
producers. I am known for having an outstanding personality, and
am frequently described as bright, intelligent, outgoing, high
energy and tenacious. I never miss landing the order! All of my
past employers have marveled at my ability to continuously
produce top flight results.

As testimony to my superior selling skills, I would like to point
out that, in past employment interviews, I have never been turned
down. It is clear to those with whom I have interviewed that I
have an awful lot to contribute to a company. I am sure that this
is why, in my last eight interviews, all of the employers have
made job offers to me.

It should be obvious to you that we should meet to discuss what
Koehler Manufacturing Company can offer an outstanding talent
like me. I am certain that you will agree that I have a lot to
contribute to Koehler, and it would be well worth your time and
effort to meet with me.

I expect to hear from you shortly.

Sincerely,

*Barbara B. Bragger*

Barbara B. Bragger

rsm

Enclosure

123 Manning Place
Bellingham, WA 29857
December 20, 1989

Mr. Oscar Bixman
Vice President of Logistics
Oxnard Cable Corporation
288 Blansford Street
Oxnard, CA 89746

Dear Mr. Bixman:

I am writing to apply for a position as corporate Distribution
Manager. I have excellent credentials in this field, and I am
sure that you will be impressed with my accomplishments, as set
forth in the enclosed resume. Read this document carefully!

I hold an M.B.A. in Materials Management from the University of
Washington, where I graduated in 1975. My undergraduate degree is
in Industrial Engineering from the same school. In both instances
I was an outstanding student, graduating with honors and serving
in a leadership capacity in several student organizations.

My professional experience includes over fourteen years in the
field of Logistics. This includes over five years as Distribution
Manager for General Manufacturing Corporation, a Fortune 200
consumer products company with annual revenues of $7.2 billion.
I am thoroughly versed in all aspects of modern distribution
methods and technology, and can bring state-of-the-art skills to
a new employer.

Let me suggest, even if you don't have a current opening in your
Distribution function, that we get together anyway. You will
likely find that I have the kind of capability that will motivate
you to consider organizational changes to accommodate me as a
member of your staff. It will become clear to you during our
forthcoming meeting that I can make significant contributions to
Oxnard Cable Corporation. We can discuss specific title and
compensation requirements at that time.

I will be calling you on Tuesday, January 3rd, to arrange for an
interview. Dates that I would have available are January 8th,
9th, 10th and 16th.

I expect to be meeting with you shortly.

Sincerely,

*Priscilla P. Pushy*

Priscilla P. Pushy

dar

Enclosure

sample G, the sentence "Read this document carefully!" is clearly offensive. It is an order rather than a polite request.

When writing a cover letter, as when writing any other business letter, you must always consider the tone in the context of the relationship between the author and the recipient. If that relationship is vendor and customer or job applicant and employer, it is important that the writer show appropriate respect for the recipient. Violating this relationship by telling the recipient what, how, or when to do something will not endear you; so be careful to avoid this tendency when writing your employment cover letter.

Here again, it is a good idea to read your letter for tone before sending it. Place yourself in the employer's shoes. How would you feel if you received this letter? Is there any wording that you would find offensive? If so, it's time to edit!

It is also a good idea to have someone else read your letter for tone. Sometimes, because you are the author, it's hard to see the forest for the trees. You may simply be too close to the work to pick up the subtleties of tone. If you cross that fine line and insult or offend the reader, you can be sure that another good employment opportunity has just gone by the wayside.

### Self-Deprecation

Some employment candidates have a facility for using the employment cover letter for "shooting themselves in the foot." Sample H is an excellent example. I call this tendency "self-deprecation."

One mainstay of the self-deprecating cover letter is the author's compulsion to point out that he or she falls short of the needed employment qualifications. Our sample cover letter does a great job of this.

Another characteristic of the self-deprecating letter is the tendency for the author to come across as shy and somewhat apologetic, as if he or she has no right to be applying for the targeted position. There is a tendency also to sound overly appreciative of the reader's consideration. Such tendencies make the candidate seem wimpish and without self-confidence—two traits of which the employer will take special notice.

It is important that you come across as someone who is confident and self-assured. It is also important that you be seen as well qualified to get the job done. Pointing out your shortcomings, acting subservient, and being wimpish will certainly not serve this purpose.

**SAMPLE H** *Poor Cover Letter*
*(Self-Deprecation)*

818 Wondering Lane
East Windsor, CT 29482
July 29, 1990

Ms Jane P. Fleishman
Manager of Public Affairs
Kellington Manufacturing Company
26 First Avenue
Philadelphia, PA 35771

Dear Ms Fleishman:

I would like to apply for a position as a Regional Lobbyist with Kellington Manufacturing Company. I hope that I have the necessary qualifications for this position.

Although I lack a full college degree and my written communication skills are not, perhaps, as good as they could be, I am a hard worker and do my best to accomplish the objectives of my employer. Sometimes I fall a little short, but usually I accomplish what has been assigned to me.

I would be very pleased if you would look favorably on my employment candidacy. I want this job very much and will work very hard if selected. I know I am not really fully qualified for this position, but I hope that you will give me a chance to demonstrate how well I can do.

Although there may be others whose education and experience make them better qualified for this position, I still hope that you will look favorably upon my resume. I hope to hear from you soon.

Thank you very much for taking the time and effort to read my resume. I appreciate this very much.

Sincerely,

*Timothy T. Timid*

Timothy T. Timid

ram

Enclosure

# 5

## ADVANCE PREPARATION

As with preparing to write the résumé or getting ready for the interview, preparation for writing an effective cover letter will clearly have a significant impact on the final outcome of your job search. If you have not taken time to prepare, your letter will likely be devoid of meaningful content and may suggest to the reader that you are somewhat shallow.

I am frequently amazed at how much time and energy are committed to writing an effective résumé, while little if any thought is given to the construction of an effective cover letter. Yet, it is almost always the cover letter that first greets the eyes of the prospective employer. It is the cover letter that either makes the sale or loses it.

Nothing kills a job search faster than a poorly prepared cover letter! If it is poorly designed, disorganized, uninteresting, full of grammatical errors and poor spelling, and so forth, in many cases the employer will not even bother to go on to the résumé, but will consign both letter and résumé to the "no interest" pile and move on to the next cover letter in the stack. The pity of this is that the candidate may have excellent employment credentials, which were set forth in a highly effective résumé; unfortunately, however, the employer never even bothered to go further than the cover letter.

By contrast, the well-written cover letter will capture the reader's interest and convince him or her that the applicant has something of value to contribute to the organization. If the letter is well constructed, the reader will feel a heightened curiosity and read the accompanying résumé with interest. In fact, if particularly well-written, the cover letter may, in some cases, even convince the reader to interview the candidate without reviewing the attendant résumé. This is, admittedly, a rare occurrence; however, it is possible.

You should think of the cover letter as you do of your appearance if you are going to meet someone you hope to impress. In this case, you will want to commit sufficient preparation time to ensure that you make a good presentation. You will want to select just the right suit or dress and accessories. Your scarf or tie will need to be just the right color and texture to complement your outfit. Your shirt or blouse will need to be clean, crisp, and well ironed  and your shoes, well shined. Your hair will need to be neatly groomed and your fingernails clean and well manicured. Everything will need to be just right to make a very favorable first impression and ensure that the relationship gets off to a good start.

Why should the cover letter be any different? Since it serves to introduce you to the employer, isn't it just as important that it be well written to ensure that this initial introduction is a favorable one? The answer to this is painfully obvious. Why, then, do so many people short-cut the cover letter writing process? I'm not really sure of the answer to this question. I do know, however, that many do short-cut this important step, and the results are frequently disastrous!

A well-written cover letter doesn't just happen. It is the product of solid advance planning and painstaking care. It is the end result of careful thought and analysis that serves to relate your specific skills and capabilities to the requirements of the position you are seeking.

## The Preparation Process

In order to write an effective cover letter, the job applicant must go through three steps. These are:

1. Job target analysis
2. Self-analysis
3. Qualifications comparison

Let's take a few moments to explore each of these important steps, which make up the "overall capability audit."

### Job Target Analysis

Since an effective cover letter will need to focus on your qualifications for the job for which you are applying, it would seem to make good sense that your cover letter preparation process start with a detailed analysis of this job. In particular, you will need to know what specific knowledge and skills will be needed for successful performance. You can bet the ranch that these are the same factors that the employer will be looking for when scanning your cover letter and résumé. Why not make the employer's job easier right from the start by highlighting these same factors in your cover letter!

Here are some questions that should help you with this job analysis step. Fill in the answers as you go.

1. What are the key functions performed or managed by this position?

_____

_____

_____

_____

_____

_____

2. What are the key ongoing functional accountabilities of this position (i.e., the key results expected for each function)?

_____

_____

_____

_____

_____

3. What are the key problems that must be solved to achieve these functional results?

_____

_____

_____

_____

_____

4. What technical knowledge is required to solve these problems and achieve the expected functional results?

A. Fields                           E. Methods/procedures

B. Disciplines                      F. Technology

C. Laws/principles/theories         G. Equipment

D. Functions                        H. Processes

_____

_____

_____

_____

_____

_____

Completion of the job analysis step should ensure that you are now focusing on the specific knowledge that will be required for this position. The next step in the advance cover letter preparation process is self-analysis.

### Self-Analysis

Now that you have completed the job analysis, your next objective should be to carefully examine your background and experience to determine how well your technical knowledge compares to the knowledge requirements of your targeted job. When completing this step, it is important to keep in mind that such knowledge is acquired in two ways:

1.  Through formal education
2.  Through experience

You must therefore carefully examine both your formal education and your professional experience to determine how this knowledge was acquired.

It is not enough simply to determine that you have the prerequisite knowledge to solve the key problems for which you will be held accountable. Employers will want to see evidence that you are able to apply this knowledge effectively and that you have achieved favorable results in the past. In behavioral interview terms, the employer will want to see behavioral evidence of your ability to achieve favorable results in those areas thought to be critical to successful job performance—that is, evidence that you are capable of successfully solving the key problems with which you will be confronted if hired for the position.

In order to successfully carry out this self-analysis step, you will have to systematically examine each facet of your background and experience to determine:

1.  Key job-related knowledge that you possess.
2.  How this knowledge was acquired.
3.  Evidence of your ability to apply this knowledge.
4.  Key results that have been achieved through application of this knowledge.

The following forms are designed to help you organize the self-evaluation process.

## Education

In the spaces provided below, fill in all information requested, starting with your most recent degree.

Degree: _____     Major: _____

What specific knowledge did you acquire that should help you solve the key problems and achieve the key functional results required of this position?

_____

_____

_____

_____

_____

_____

Degree: _____ Major:_____

What specific knowledge did you acquire that should help you solve the key problems and achieve the key functional results required of this position?

_____

_____

_____

_____

_____

_____

## Training

Beyond your formal education, what additional training courses or seminars have you attended that have provided you with job-relevant knowledge in those areas previously identified as critical to successful job performance?

Course/seminar attended: _____

Key knowledge acquired: _____

_____

_____

_____

_____

Course/seminar attended: _____

Key knowledge acquired: _____

_____

_____

_____

_____

Course/seminar attended: _____

Key knowledge acquired: _____

_____

_____

_____

_____

Use additional paper, if required, to complete this analysis of your relevant training courses and seminars. Be sure that you are concentrating only on those that have helped you develop specific knowledge that is important to solving the key functional problems for which you will be accountable in your target position. Avoid any training that is not relevant to this position.

## Work Experience

Analysis of your professional experience, in most cases, will be the most important part of the self-analysis process. It is here that you will have the opportunity to identify your specific achievements and results in those functional areas for which you will be accountable in the new position. Such achievements and results provide convincing evidence to prospective employers of your ability to solve important job-related problems and achieve required functional results. They provide tangible proof of your ability to be "value adding" to the new organization.

To start this process, review past positions you have held to determine which are most closely related to your target job. Which of these positions have had the same or similar functional accountabilities as those in the target position? Which have required you to solve problems similar to those you will face in the new position? Include in your analysis only those having functional accountabilities and problems similar to your target position. Nonrelated positions should be skipped.

Complete the following information for each relevant position:

Position Title: _____

Company     : _____

Division     : _____

Department  : _____

Key functional accountabilities: _____

_____

_____

_____

_____

_____

Key functional results achieved: _____

_____

_____

_____

_____

_____

_____

Time in position: _____

Position title : _____

Company      : _____

Department   : _____

Key functional accountabilities: _____

_____

_____

_____

_____

_____

_____

Key functional results achieved: _____

_____

_____

_____

_____

_____

Time in position: _____

Position title : _____

Company    : _____

Department  : _____

Key functional accountabilities: _____

_____

_____

_____

_____

_____

Key functional results achieved: _____

_____

_____

_____

_____

_____

Time in Position: _____

Use additional paper if you need more space to complete this analysis.

Analysis of your relevant work history should provide you with an excellent list of target job related accomplishments from which to choose as you begin to design your cover letter. Because you have taken the time to complete the analysis, this information will be at your fingertips when you need it.

### Qualifications Analysis

I am sure that having completed both the position analysis and your self-analysis, you have become keenly aware of many specific examples of how your education, training, and experience have prepared you to carry out the functional responsibilities of your target position and achieve the key functional results that prospective employers will expect of you. More important, if you have been thorough, you have likely identified significant results that you have achieved that offer convincing evidence of your ability to solve the key functional problems confronted by these prospective employers. Citing such achievements in the cover letter can be a powerful tool in persuading employers of your ability to be a major value-adding contributor to their organizations. It can form the very heart of an effective cover letter.

After the position analysis and self-analysis, the next step in the cover letter advance preparation process is the qualifications comparison. The intent of this process is threefold:

1.  To determine where your qualifications and the requirements of the target position overlap.
2.  To determine the functional priorities of target companies.
3.  To allow you to select the achievements compatible with these functional priorities that will have the most impact.

The following set of questions should help you with this process and allow you to narrow the field down to those achievements that will have the most favorable impact on the companies you have targeted in your job search.

1.  Of the various functions for which your target position is responsible which are probably the most important from the standpoint of overall organizational success? (Arrange these in order of organizational impact).

_____

_____

_____

_____

2. What are the desired functional results required for overall organizational success for each of the above priority functions? (List these
   results in the same order as above).

_____

_____

_____

_____

3. Using the self-analysis data previously developed, list the most significant results you have achieved that correspond to the desired
   functional results listed in question 2.

_____

_____

_____

_____

_____

_____

   You have now completed your overall capability audit and have developed the kind of information you will need to design effective cover

letters. This should save you considerable time as it becomes necessary throughout your job hunting campaign to write various kinds of cover letters. Also important, it will allow you to highlight those accomplishments and qualifications most related to the critical functional needs of the employer. These are the ones that will do the most to promote your job search interests by positioning you as a key contributor in those areas most important to organizational success. This approach is sure to convince most employers that you have what it takes for successful job performance and that your employment candidacy is well worth pursuing.

# 6

# COVER LETTER
# INCLUSIONS/EXCLUSIONS

What kind of information should be included in the cover letter? Or, perhaps more important, what information is better left out? This is one of the frequent dilemmas faced by the cover letter author.

If you were recently laid off, should you offer an explanation in the cover letter? If you have held several previous jobs with numerous employers, should you offer an explanation for your frequent movement? Should you attempt to explain employment gaps in your résumé? How about physical handicaps or serious health problems? Should these be discussed in the cover letter?

These and similar questions are the topic of this chapter. We will attempt to provide you with some guidelines for answering them and for deciding what type of information is truly beneficial to the objectives of the cover letter. Conversely, we will also discuss criteria for deciding what kind of information may detract from cover letter effectiveness and thus should best be excluded. Let's examine these categories one at a time.

### Job Objective

Generally, it is felt that a statement of your employment interest, including job objective, should be included in the first paragraph of the cover letter. This conveys to the reader the intent of your letter and serves to focus his or her attention on your qualifications. Here are some examples of introductory paragraphs that include a job objective statement:

*Enclosed please find my résumé for your review. I am interested in applying for a position as purchasing agent with Barron Chemical, and would appreciate your consideration of my employment credentials.*

*I am seeking a responsible position in R&D management requiring a Ph.D. with 15 years of experience and proven skills in polymer and specialty chemical research.*

*As President of a leading firm in the electronics field, you are aware, I am sure, of the importance and value of a top flight Chief Financial Officer. If you are in the market for such an individual, you may wish to give serious consideration to my credentials.*

If you do not include a statement of your job objective near the beginning of the cover letter, you will fail to focus the reader's attention on the reason for your letter. To simply state that you are interested in employment, without specifying your job objective, can leave the impression that you are vague, indirect, or indecisive, or all three. It may also suggest to the employer that you are somewhat desperate for employment and, consequently, will accept any old thing. These are certainly not the impressions that you want to create in your cover letter.

On the other hand, the inclusion of a job objective in the beginning paragraph adds focus to your cover letter. It helps to establish the reason for your letter and focuses the reader's attention on your credentials for such an assignment. It also suggests to the employer that you are organized, direct, focused, and businesslike in your approach. These are far more desirable descriptors.

In stating an employment objective, however, you should be particularly careful in choosing your words. If the objective provides too narrow a description, it may cause you to be screened out from consideration for positions that may, in fact, be of interest to you. If described too broadly, on the other hand, the objective may suggest that you are vague and indecisive. Here are some examples:

*I am seeking a senior-level accounting or financial position with broad management responsibility for achievement of the company's financial objectives.*

*I seek a position with responsibility for overall direction of the financial planning function.*

*I am looking for a good career position with your organization.*

The first objective is worded rather broadly and suggests that the candidate is receptive to a wide range of financial and accounting positions (including financial planning). The second objective is a bit more confining and limits employment consideration to financial planning only. This suggests that the candidate would not consider other related financial and accounting positions, thus serving to screen him or her out from consideration for such positions. Finally, the third objective is unusually vague and fails to provide the desired focus necessary to an effective cover letter.

You can see from these examples that the wording of the objective statement is of considerable importance. You will need to word your statement with great care so that you focus the reader's attention but don't screen yourself out from opportunities that you may wish to consider.


## Reason for Job Search

Some cover letter authors feel compelled to offer the employer an explanation for their job search. This is particularly true if their separation from their last employer was the result of a layoff or company downsizing program.

Many writers include such an explanation in response to what I call "historical guilt." In the old days (i.e., 15 to 20 or so years ago), there was a lot of social stigma attached to being unemployed. Unemployment suggested that you were unstable, lazy, unreliable, and otherwise unable to hold a job. If you had been previously employed, current unemployment, in many cases, also suggested that you had been fired. As a result, people who were legitimately laid off felt compelled to differentiate their circumstances from the "socially undesirable" by offering an explanation for their employment separation. Today, this is no longer the case.

The recent rash of corporate downsizings throughout the United States has served to separate a number of good performers from the corporate ranks. Most of these downsizing efforts have been "voluntary" programs offering various financial incentives for voluntary resignation from the company. Some of these programs have offered up to a year's pay or more to encourage employee resignation—often sufficient incentive to allow frustrated but otherwise good performers to gracefully exit the organization.

The ranks of the unemployed today contain a number of good workers, and most employers are well aware of this fact. There is, therefore, considerably less social stigma attached to being unemployed, and employers are less likely to associate unemployment with laziness, instability, or poor performance. Unless the period of unemployment has been of considerable duration (i.e., a year or more), therefore, you should not feel compelled to offer an explanation in the cover letter. If you feel that you "must" do so, however, here are some ways to accomplish this.

*A recent decision by the Baxtor Corporation to shut down its Wexler Division has necessitated my current job search.*

*I have recently elected to participate in Darrow Corporation's voluntary separation program for the purpose of pursuing more promising career options.*

*As a key executive in the appliance manufacturing field, you are aware, I am sure, of Brighton Corporation's decision to close its Wayne Narrows Plant. As a consequence of this decision, I am currently seeking a responsible position as a Director of Manufacturing.*

In general, unless you feel compelled to do so, I recommend that you not include such explanations. Since the purpose of your cover letter is to sell the employer on the idea of interviewing you, such explanations are seldom beneficial to this objective. To the contrary, they tend to take up valuable space that might be more constructively used to market your skills and overall capability. I believe that the issue of past job separations is usually better handled at the employment interview.

## Explanation of Employment Gaps

If your résumé contains employment gaps, you may or may not want to use the cover letter to provide an explanation. Generally, however, unless there is an acceptable reason for these gaps, such explanations are best left out. They only serve as a "red flag" that draws the reader's attention away from your positive qualifications as an employment candidate. Why highlight this potentially negative information in your cover letter?

I would also not attempt to explain employment gaps in the résumé. Why make it easy for the employer to spot them? At least, by excluding this information, you may have the opportunity to discuss the matter during the employment interview. By then, however, you have also had an opportunity to counter this potential negative by effectively marketing your ability to make contributions to the hiring organization. Should you volunteer an explanation of these gaps in advance, you may never even have the opportunity for an interview with the employer.

So, in final analysis, my recommendation is, don't volunteer this information—let the employer ask.

## Compensation

Should you list compensation history or compensation requirements in the cover letter? It all depends upon the circumstances.

Generally, the inclusion of salary information does not add much to the cover letter. And it can serve to focus the reader's attention on cost rather than on the value you can bring to the organization. This is particularly true if your current pay level is considered high for your position, background, and years of experience. Sensitivity, of course, diminishes if your current compensation level places you in the lower level of a prospective employer's salary range.

Another argument against including salary information in the cover letter relates to the space it requires. Due to the limited space available in the cover letter, it is generally felt that this same space might be more effectively used to market your qualifications and overall value.

Another factor to consider, when determining whether to include salary information, is your current employment status. If you are comfortably employed and are in a position to wait until just the right opportunity comes along, there is a lot less to lose if you are screened out because of salary requirements. In such cases, you may want to state your requirements in the letter, since this could serve your interests by screening out lower-paying opportunities that do not fit your needs.

On the other hand, if you have been unemployed for a lengthy period of time and are feeling somewhat desperate, listing your salary requirements in the cover letter could screen you out from opportunities that you might later wish you had pursued. By excluding salary information, you may at least afford yourself the opportunity to find out more about the position with a prospective employer. Armed with information not only about the immediate opening but also about such things as future advancement opportunities and the company's benefits program, you could well be happy that you didn't allow yourself to be screened from consideration.

Sometimes people whose salaries are particularly low by comparative standards may feel that listing their compensation level in the cover letter will induce employers to pursue their candidacy. Although this may work in some cases, in others, it may backfire. For example, an unusually low salary can be a red flag to certain employers, causing them to question just how competent and qualified the candidate is. Obviously, there must be something wrong!

The general rule of thumb suggested by most employment experts is, don't volunteer either salary history or compensation requirements in the cover letter unless specifically asked by the employer to furnish this information. Even in those cases where you have been asked to state compensation requirements, try to avoid being too specific. In responding to such requests, it is usually best to cite a range—for example, mid-$40K range or low-$60K range. By doing this, you are not automatically screening yourself out, and you are still preserving some flexibility for future salary negotiations.

## Job Hopping

The job hopper is someone who simply has had too many employers in too short a time. Should the job hopper use the cover letter to offer some explanation for the number of moves made? Let's explore this question in some detail.

Although there is no set standard, it is well known that having too many jobs in too short a time can be very detrimental to a job search. What might be considered an excessive number of employers in one industry, however, may be considered average in another. For example, those who work as engineers for engineering job shops or contract engineering firms are frequently subject to layoffs. If the economy is healthy and firms are engaged in hefty capital expansion projects, engineering contractors can't get enough engineers. On the other hand, when the economy contracts and capital expansion dries up, it's layoff time.

Firms engaged in contract engineering and similar industries that are heavily affected by swings in the economic cycle are accustomed to seeing several moves on an individual's résumé. But industries that are less volatile would expect to see fewer employment changes. So, what constitutes the job stability standard in one industry may be totally different from the standard in another.

Further confusing this topic is the fact that there are many reasons why an individual changes employers. Some of them are considered "acceptable" in the eyes of the employment professional; others are deemed "unacceptable." Here are some examples:

*Acceptable Reasons*

1. Elimination of job
2. Elimination of function/department
3. Company-wide layoff
4. Voluntary resignation as part of downsizing
5. Company acquisition and subsequent layoff

6. Nepotism—replaced by relative of owner
7. Health

*Unacceptable Reasons*

1. Poor performance
2. Incompatibility with management/fellow workers
3. Absenteeism
4. Dishonesty
5. Quitting without notice

Although it should be obvious that you should not use the cover letter to highlight unacceptable reasons for past terminations, how about those cases where such termination was for acceptable reasons? Should this information be volunteered in the cover letter to distinguish you from those who have been involuntarily terminated for unacceptable reasons?

In general, regardless of reason, it is recommended that the job hunter not use the cover letter to offer explanations for job hopping. This only highlights the problem and detracts from the candidate's presentation of overall skills and capabilities. In fact, if the job applicant can do a sufficient job of marketing his or her ability to add value to the organization, the prospective employer may be willing to overlook past transgressions. Instead of highlighting these past moves in the cover letter, therefore, I recommend that the problem of job hopping be dealt with in another medium—namely, the résumé.

The problem can be best addressed by choosing a résumé format that emphasizes skills and accomplishments and deemphasizes employment chronology. Thus, the job hunter should choose a functional rather than a chronological résumé format. A well-prepared functional résumé will focus the employer's attention on skills and accomplishments rather than on periods of employment. For further information on how to prepare an effective functional résumé, you might want to consult my book, *The Resume Kit* (Wiley, 1984).

## Experience Deficit

If you lack prerequisite experience to qualify for your job objective, should this lack be addressed in the cover letter? My advice here is similar to that offered in the discussion of job hopping.

By using the cover letter to discuss the fact that you do not possess the prerequisite experience required for a given position, you are substantially detracting from your employment candidacy in the eyes of the employer. Why highlight this fact in the cover letter, giving the employer every reason to screen you out? Why not let the employer discover this independently? Why make it easy and destroy whatever chances you might have had to convince the employer that you are a candidate worth considering?

If you think about the fundamentals of the employment decision-making process from the employer's viewpoint, you will likely conclude that the employer is hiring someone on the basis of ability to solve certain key problems and make certain key contributions—not on the basis of past experience. The focus is therefore on whether you possess certain knowledge and skills and can effectively apply them to the areas of concern to the prospective employer. Although not frequently, I have witnessed employers totally abandon specific experience requirements in the interests of hiring a particular candidate who, they felt, had excellent skills in those areas critical to successful job performance.

With this in mind, don't jeopardize your chances for employment by highlighting your lack of specific experience in the cover letter. Instead, use the cover letter to effectively market your skills and capabilities (as well as your desire and motivation) to make substantive contributions to the employer.

Here again, the functional résumé format can be used, in conjunction with the skills-focused cover letter, to reinforce your qualifications for the position you seek. This format, rather than the chronological résumé format, will enable you to focus the employer's attention on your overall skills and capabilities rather than on past work experience. The skills-focused letter and the functional résumé, in combination, can complement each other nicely, providing some pretty convincing evidence of your potential for successful job performance.

## Educational Deficit

For purposes of our discussion, the term "educational deficit" means a lack of the educational qualifications normally required by most employers when filling a given professional position. Most employers attempting to fill an engineering position will require a degree in engineering; likewise, when filling a position in market research, most will require an M.B.A. in marketing. Many other examples could easily be cited where the requirement for certain educational credentials might be considered ironclad.

As with an experience deficit, it is recommended that you not attempt to explain away a specific educational deficit in your cover letter. It is generally best that it not be mentioned in the cover letter at all—why underline it by volunteering its existence? What real purpose does this serve? If anything, it will likely screen you from consideration before the employer has had a chance to review your other qualifications in the accompanying résumé. This is particularly important when you have had direct experience in the field for which you are applying and can, as a result, graphically demonstrate your ability to successfully perform the job.

Under these circumstances, it is far more important to use the cover letter to focus the reader's attention on specific accomplishments and results achieved that are directly related to the position for which you are applying. You can thus provide a convincing argument supporting your ability to make valuable contributions to the hiring organization. For most employers, this is far more important than the specifics of one's educational background.

Sure, your candidacy is somewhat handicapped by not having the specific educational credentials normally sought for such positions. But this may be far from fatal depending upon what evidence you can cite concerning your ability to meet the major requirements of the position. After all, knowledge is acquired by means other than formal education. It can just as easily be acquired through informal training and actual job experience. Job experience, in particular, can provide invaluable education that has benefits far beyond those normally acquired in the formal classroom. After all, it is the actual job environment that tests your ability to apply your knowledge. Simply having the formal education is not enough if you are unable to successfully apply what you have learned.

So, in final analysis, you should avoid bringing this educational deficit to an employer's attention in the cover letter. Furthermore, when designing the résumé that will accompany your cover letter, be sure to obscure your educational credentials by listing them near the bottom of the second page rather than prominently displaying them at the beginning. I have seen many highly successful people who, on the basis of their educational credentials alone, would not survive the employment screening process.

## Physical Handicap or Serious Illness

If you have a physical handicap or a chronic serious illness, should you mention this fact in the cover letter? This is not an easy question to answer and requires a bit of discussion.

Generally, the guidelines I recommend for making this determination are related to two things:

1. The severity of the condition
2. Your level of social confidence

If the severity of your condition is such that it would have little bearing upon your ability to perform the job in question, my advice is clear: Don't bring the subject up in your cover letter. Instead, assuming you feel compelled to bring this to the employer's attention at all, wait until the hiring process has proceeded to the point that the employer has made clear his or her strong interest in you. It is at this point that your condition is least likely to have a negative impact on your chances of being hired. The employer is already convinced that you have what it takes to successfully contribute to the organization and will be more likely to overlook this issue than if confronted with it at the outset of the screening process.

If you are suffering from a chronic condition that will clearly affect your ability to perform the job, again, I would not mention this fact in the cover letter, especially if some sort of reasonable accommodation can be provided (i.e., special desk, chair, device, etc.) that will allow you to function normally. Unfortunately, such mention will, in many cases, automatically screen you from further consideration.

Here again, it is better to wait until the interview to address this topic. At least you will have gained the opportunity to present your credentials and convince the employer that you can be a valuable contributor despite your handicap or medical condition. If you are successful in marketing your overall qualifications and capabilities during the interview, perhaps the conversation can then turn to providing the necessary support and accommodations you need to sustain your job performance at a consistently high level.

An important consideration when deciding whether to mention your handicap in the cover letter is your level of social comfort. If you are fairly comfortable with your handicap and will not be embarrassed by the interviewer's potential surprise or awkwardness, by all means, do not mention your handicap in the cover letter. On the other hand, if you are severely handicapped and feel compelled to advise the employer of this, then do so.

Should you elect to discuss your handicap or medical condition in the cover letter, be sure to provide sufficient information. Don't keep the employer guessing about your ability to perform the job. This discussion should give a fairly detailed and accurate description of your physical limitations and how they relate to your ability to function.

Don't overdo it, however. Remember, the employer is really interested in your job qualifications. It is important, therefore, that you offer a convincing presentation of your qualifications and your interest in the job. First generate interest in your candidacy, and then, having accomplished this, introduce the subject of your handicap, along with a frank description of your limitations and some convincing evidence showing that they will not substantially affect your ability to perform the major duties of the job for which you are applying.

I hope this chapter has answered most of your important questions concerning the kinds of information that should be included in or excluded from your employment cover letter. Some of these matters are rather delicate and will require careful handling if you are to put your best foot forward and end up with that critical employment interview. Carefully consider the content of your cover letter, therefore, to be sure that you maximize your opportunities for presenting your case to the employer on a face-to-face basis. Be sure not to include unnecessary topics that may screen you out before you even have a chance to get started.

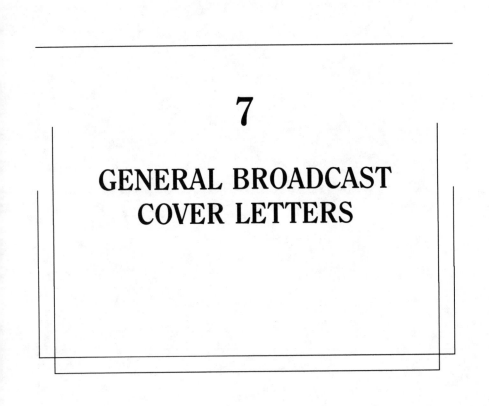

# 7

# GENERAL BROADCAST COVER LETTERS

The general broadcast cover letter is the kind used by the job seeker to mass-mail his or her résumé to a large number of prospective employers. Although commonly used, the direct mail campaign is not known to be a highly productive employment technique. In a successful direct mail campaign, the response rate will normally run in the 2 to 5 percent range. Most employment candidates should consider themselves quite fortunate to realize this kind of response.

Probably, the single factor accounting for this low level of response from the direct mail campaign is competition. It is not uncommon for the corporate employment department of a major corporation, for example, to receive 40,000 to 50,000 résumés a year. Some of the more sought-after large corporations, in fact, are known to receive well over 100,000 employment inquiries a year.

Compounding this problem of volume competition has been the "skinnying down" process many employers have gone through in recent years. In an effort to become more cost competitive, they have substantially cut the size of their workforces. Cuts in the 20 to 30 percent range are not uncommon, with staff functions such as the employment department being reduced by as much as 50 percent.

Given the volume of employment inquiries received by these employers, coupled with substantially reduced staffing of their employment departments, it is not difficult to understand why the direct mail campaign is not a highly productive job hunting technique. If read at all, unsolicited employment inquiries receive only a cursory review. There is simply not the time or the manpower to warrant a more thorough approach.

This does not mean that you should avoid using the direct mail technique as part of your job search. To the contrary, this technique is considered to be a standard in every well-planned employment campaign. Although it requires considerable work for the level of anticipated result, it should be kept in mind that just one favorable response resulting from a well-orchestrated direct mail campaign has the potential to provide you with an excellent job offer and an exciting career opportunity. Due to the low response rate, however, it should not be considered the cornerstone of your employment strategy.

### Target Companies

It is not uncommon for employment candidates to target several hundred companies for their direct mail lists. Sometimes, they may include as many as 500 to 600. However, the direct mail list usually consists of what I call the "second tier" companies. It should not include the 10 or 20 "primary" target companies for which you would most like to work. These companies should be singled out for a much more tailored, customized approach (including individual research) than that offered by the direct mail campaign.

The number of companies included in the target list for the direct mail campaign makes it impractical to conduct individual company research; so the cover letter used is less focused and must be designed to appeal to a much broader audience. It will not be possible to design a single letter that addresses the specific needs of such a large list of employers. A different tack is required.

## Generic Results

Since the number of companies to be included in the direct mail campaign is simply too large to allow a tailored, needs-focused approach, the cover letter to be used will need to be more generic. By this I mean that it must be designed to appeal to the generic, or common, needs of all companies.

As discussed earlier, employers don't fill jobs just for the sake of filling them. Instead, they expect to fill their openings with persons they think are capable of achieving certain results and thereby adding value to the organization. Therefore, good cover letter design requires that the letter, as well as the accompanying résumé, highlight your ability to contribute specific results to the prospective employer's organization.

A mere summary of your education and employment history does not really accomplish this. Such a summary simply states your general qualifications; it doesn't highlight the contributions you can make and the value you can bring to the firm. To be persuasive and convince an employer that you are someone worth pursuing, you will need to focus the employer's attention on the kind of results that can be expected if you are hired. The best way to do this is to use the cover letter to highlight some of the key results you have accomplished for employers in the past.

If you are looking back over a number of years of employment, you may find it difficult to decide which past results to highlight. The best way to make this decision is to determine which are most relevant to the type of position for which you are applying. Here are some questions that may help you with this process:

1. What are the key generic responsibilities of the position for which you are applying?
2. If these responsibilities are met, what specific results would you expect to see?
3. What similar job responsibilities have you had in the past?
4. What were the major results and accomplishments you achieved in these key areas of responsibility?

In answering these questions, you will likely find that the kind of responsibilities and results identified are fairly common, or generic, to the job function. These appear to be universal, regardless of the employer. Here are some examples of what I mean:

Function            : *Manufacturing*
Key accountability : Produce highest-quality product at lowest possible cost.
Valued results      : Increased quality
                      Reduced scrap
                      Reduced costs (labor/material)
                      Increased output
Function            : *Marketing*
Key accountability : Increase sales volume and market share with minimum investment and maximum return.
Valued results      : Increased sales volume
                      Increased market share
                      Increased penetration—existing market
                      New market penetration
                      Reduced advertising expense
Function            : *Human Resources*
Key accountability : Increase organizational productivity through improved planning, selection, development, and motivation of employees.
Valued results      : Reduced employee turnover
                      No labor strikes
                      Improved employee attendance
                      Reduced work-related injuries
                      Increased production per employee

As you can see, these valued results are generic. They are expected of the functional specialty in which one works, regardless of the employer or the employer's work. These are common results that all employers consider highly desirable; so if you choose to highlight them in a general broadcast cover letter, you will be focusing on values that have universal appeal.

Review of the sample cover letters at the end of this chapter will reveal that these results or contributions can be presented in either linear or paragraph form. Sample A is an example of the linear approach. Here, each key result or accomplishment is highlighted on a separate line. Sample D, on the other hand, highlights these accomplishments in paragraph form. In my judgment, the linear approach is more effective, since each accomplishment is presented on a separate line and is therefore more visible.

## Skills and Attributes Focus

A recent graduate, who has no prior relevant work experience, will not be able to cite specific work-related accomplishments. In such instances, a different approach is required in the cover letter. He or she can emphasize specific technical skills and personal attributes thought to be important to good job performance. Cover letter sample B is an example of such an approach.

In Sample B, Donald Bassett, an upcoming graduate of Bucknell University, is using his cover letter to apply for a position as a sales trainee with The Linton Company. Since Don has no appropriate sales experience, he chooses to highlight personal accomplishments and attributes that he feels are important to good performance as a sales professional. Some of these are:

- Interest and enthusiasm
- Outgoing, friendly personality
- Enjoy developing strong personal relationships
- Bias for action
- Strong service orientation
- Drive and determination
- Leadership
- Energy

Don's letter is particularly well-written, and it serves to relate some of these personal attributes to specific results desired of good sales professionals.

## Cover Letter Elements

Review of the sample cover letters at the end of this chapter suggests that there are certain elements that are common to most general broadcast letters. These are:

1. Block or full block format
2. Address of a specific hiring executive
3. Introductory paragraph including statement of objective
4. Statement of relevant accomplishments
5. Brief background summary
6. Request for action
7. Statement of appreciation

Let's take a few moments to discuss each of these elements so that you can fully appreciate their role in and their overall importance to the effectiveness of your cover letter.

As is the case with other cover letters discussed in this book, the formats recommended for the general broadcast cover letter are block and full block. Both are widely used and accepted designs that increase ease of reading and present an overall neat, organized appearance. These formats are discussed in great detail in Chapter 2, so I will not discuss them further here.

You will note that each of the sample letters in this chapter is addressed to a specific executive by both name and title. In each case, he or she has broad management responsibilities for the function in which the job applicant has interest, and is normally also responsible for making hiring decisions for that function.

When targeting functional executives, it is important to select those who are managerially at the proper level to have interest in your background. The rule of thumb is to select those who are organizationally two levels above the position for which you are applying. Such individuals are usually not only aware of specific openings for which you might qualify, but may also be considering the possibility of replacing the individual who might have been your new boss.

By applying at this level, you may increase your chances for employment at more than one level in the organization. Additionally, if your would-be boss is handed your cover letter and résumé by his or her boss, along with favorable comments on your candidacy, this may result in a more thorough review of your credentials than might otherwise have been the case. Also, your cover letter and accompanying résumé may be just the ticket that convinces the senior manager to approve that employment requisition your would-be boss has been seeking.

As previously stated, whenever possible, you should avoid sending your cover letter to the company's Personnel or Employment functions, since they are often aware only of current openings and may be totally unaware of the line executive's future staffing requirements. Additionally, because he or she may lack specific knowledge of your functional specialty, the Personnel or Employment Manager may not be fully qualified to judge the value of your technical credentials.

In all cases, it is strongly recommended that you address your cover letter to a specific individual rather than to a functional area. To do otherwise is to further increase the impersonal nature of an already somewhat impersonal correspondence. This will surely cause your star to fall considerably in the eyes of the employer. It suggests that you do not have the intelligence, resourcefulness, or motivation to do the minimal research usually required to uncover this information.

Although the volume of the direct mail campaign will not permit the design of a tailored, personalized introductory paragraph in your cover letter, nonetheless, you should try to make it as interesting as possible in an effort to stimulate readership. The sample cover letters at the end of this chapter should give you some ideas in this regard. Where possible, try to create some curiosity about your qualifications and ability to contribute to the hiring company. Additionally, adopt a businesslike tone and state your interest in employment with the firm.

As the samples will show, your letter should also contain a brief summary of your overall credentials. Normally, this includes the following:

1.  Job-relevant degree and major
2.  Number of years of job-related functional experience
3.  Some statement implying your success in this function

If your major is unrelated to the position for which you are applying, a simple statement of degree level (excluding major) will be sufficient.

In fact, in such cases, mention of the major may be to your detriment, suggesting to some employers that you don't have the necessary formal education to support your job objective.

Additionally, if you include a statement of your years of experience, be sure not to overdo it. If you are moving into the twilight years of your career, highlighting your 30 or 40 years of experience may be just what the employer needs to practice age discrimination and screen you out before you can even get started. Likewise, if your years of experience seem unusually heavy for the level of the position for which you are applying, this may raise some unnecessary red flags. In such cases, simply state that you have "excellent experience" in the field, excluding any reference to the number of years.

In reviewing the sample general broadcast cover letters found at the end of this chapter, you will also discover that another common element they share is the statement of job-relevant accomplishments, presented in either linear or paragraph form. Since this topic has been discussed in detail earlier in this chapter, we will not belabor the point here. Suffice it to say that the statement of job-relevant accomplishments is an essential element of the cover letter, which serves to market your value-adding capabilities to the prospective employer. This element is key to the effectiveness of your cover letter and should therefore be considered an integral part of your design.

Most well-designed cover letters will include an action-motivating statement of some sort in the last or second-to-last paragraph. This statement either requests action on the part of the employer or states that the author intends to take further action as a follow-up to the correspondence. The sample cover letters illustrate several techniques for accomplishing this. In each case, the action-motivating statement is intended to motivate the employer to contact the applicant or to prepare the employer for future contact by the author. In either case, it is used to keep the relationship moving toward the letter's objective—a job interview.

The final common element of an effective general broadcast cover letter is a statement of appreciation. This is an act of common courtesy and reflects favorably on your good manners and consideration of others. Simply put, this statement thanks the reader for the time that he or she has invested in reviewing your employment credentials. Such sensitivity to the reader's time will usually reflect well on your candidacy.

The remainder of this chapter contains sample general broadcast cover letters for your perusal. You should find them helpful for designing your own broadcast letter.

825 Hawk Road
Wellsville, WA 82734
April 30, 1995

Ms Phyliss E. Beaseley
Director of Marketing
Morton Foods Company
100 Hot Water Drive
Lancaster, OH 28476

Dear Ms Beaseley:

I am writing to present my credentials for the position of Brand
Manager, a position for which I am exceptionally well-qualified.
I am confident that you will quickly realize my ability to make
major contributions to Morton Foods' marketing efforts upon
reviewing the enclosed resume.

It should be obvious from my resume, that I have an outstanding
record for pumping new life into old brands and making them hum.
Examples of my accomplishments include:

- Increased Kem market share by 99% in two years

- Doubled Tonkin market share in 9 months

- Improved direct mail response on Leggins brand by
  28% in 18 months

My contributions to new brands have been equally impressive. For
example:

- Developed 20% market share penetration in Sheer Magic
  within one year of market introduction

- Completed national roll-out of Star Gazer in 9 months,
  with 18% market penetration

Perhaps I can make similar contribution to Morton Foods in the
marketing of either new or existing brands.

My backgound includes an M.B.A. in Marketing from the Harvard
Business School, plus over fifteen years experience in Market
Research and Marketing.

Should you have room in your organization for a top-notch
marketing professional who can make immediate contributions to
your marketing efforts and add profit to your bottom line, I can
be reached at (312) 287-3957 during the day and (312) 873-2917
during evenings and weekends. I look forward to your call.

Thank you for your consideration.

Sincerely,

*Craig B. Johnston*

Craig B. Johnston

hdr

Enclosure

## SAMPLE B *General Broadcast Letter*

125 Schwartz Hall
Bucknell University
Lewisberg, PA 18775
January 5, 1992

Mr. Steven Becker
Director of Sales and Marketing
The Linton Company
133 Republic Square
Dayton, OH 17385

Dear Mr. Becker:

I am submitting my resume for your review for the position of
Sales Representative Trainee with The Linton Company. I feel
that I have the necessary qualifications for your serious
consideration and would appreciate the opportunity to
demonstrate this through a personal interview with your
recruiter during your upcoming interview schedule at Bucknell.

Although short on experience, I am long on interest and
enthusiasm! I am an outgoing, friendly individual who would
enjoy developing strong personal relationships with customers.
My bias for action and strong service orientation would serve me
particularly well in responding to the needs of client
organizations. My drive, determination and leadership skills are
well evidenced by the following accomplishments:

  - Grade Point Average of 3.6/4.0

  - Fraternity President in Senior Year
    Fraternity Vice President in Junior Year
    Pledge Chairman in Sophomore Year

  - Captain of Varsity Football Team - Senior Year
    Varsity Football - 4 years
    Varsity Tennis   - 3 years
    Intramural Wrestling & Boxing

  - Producer & Director - Fraternity Play

I would like the chance to put my energy, drive and enthusiasm
to work for a company such as yours. May I have the opportunity
to further discuss my interest and qualifications during a
personal interview with your representative?

I will call you on Wednesday, January 15, to determine your
interest and to arrange a suitable time for a meeting with your
recruiter. Thank you for your consideration.

Sincerely,

*Donald K. Bassett*

Donald K. Bassett
Student

sab

Enclosure

325 Serenity Lane
Lawndale, GA 82739
May 15, 1990

Mr. George R. Worthing, Jr.
President
Barrington Corporation
1835 North C Street
Williamsville, NC 29876

Dear Mr. Worthing:

As the senior executive of a leading company in the field of copper tubing, I am sure that you are well aware of the difference that a top-notch manufacturing executive can make to a company's bottom line. If you are currently seeking a proven contributor as a senior executive to lead your manufacturing operations, I encourage you to consider my credentials.

As a manufacturing executive, with a M.S. degree in Engineering and over 15 years of progressively responsible assignments, I have established a record as a substantive contributor to the profitability of my employers. Among some of my more notable achievements are:

- a 32% reduction in manufacturing costs in a major furnace operation (annual savings of $9 million)

- on time and below cost start-up of a $345 million tube manufacturing plant (project savings of $19 million)

- a 26% reduction in labor costs over three plant operations through creative reorganization and training program (annual savings of $6 million)

- installation of a Deming-based total quality program that reduced scrap by 68% and customer complaints by 86% (estimated annual savings of $3 million)

If you are interested in meeting to explore how I might be able to contribute to the Barrington Corporation, I can be reached during evenings and weekends at (413) 872-1987. I can also be reached during business hours at (413) 734-9982, with discretion.

Thank you for your consideration.

Sincerely yours,

*Stephen R. Joppal*

Stephen R. Joppal

gth

Enclosure

**SAMPLE D** *General Broadcast Letter*

130 Sheldon Lane
Rochester, NY 87392
March 15, 1995

Ms Martha Remington
Vice President of Research
Seabright Chemical Company
133 South Barring Street
Westville, NJ 18372

Dear Ms Remington:

As one of the leaders in the field of polymer chemistry,
Seabright Chemical Company might be interested in a seasoned
Product Development Chemist with a demonstrated record of
achievement in successful new product innovation. My credentials
include an M.S. degree in Polymer Chemistry with 15 years of
experience and proven skills in polymer and specialty chemical
research.

As you can see from the enclosed resume, my reputation as a
creative, innovative scientist is well supported by 26 register-
ed patents and 22 new product introductions. Perhaps I can make
similar contributions to your company.

I have extensive experience and can make substantive contributions in the following chemical specialties:

    Organic & Polymer Specialty Chemicals
        - Water Treatment Chemicals
        - Oil Field and Mining Chemicals
        - Consumer Products Based on Water Soluble Polymers

    Polymers, Rubbers and Plastics
        - New Polymers and Plastics - Synthetic Approach
        - New Polymers and Plastics - Physio-Chemical Approach

My current salary is $72K, and I have no geographical
restrictions.

Should you have an appropriate position available on your
Research staff, I would welcome the opportunity to personally
discuss how I might meaningfully contribute to your product
development efforts. I can be reached at (325) 534-9837 during
the day and at (325) 564-2975 during evenings and weekends.

Thank you for your consideration, and I look forward to hearing
from you.

Sincerely,

*Michael D. Harrison*

Michael D. Harrison

rfk

Enclosure

132 East Liberty Street
San Francisco, CA 28736
September 23, 1990


Mr. Samuel R. Bothum
Vice President of Engineering
Worthington Corporation
100 East Waverly Street
Atlanta, GA 19738


Dear Mr. Bothum:

I am writing to express my interest in a position as Senior
Project Engineer with Worthington Corporation. Review of the
enclosed resume will reveal that I have had strong project
experience with The Johnson Company, one of your key
competitors.

My background includes a B.S. degree in Mechanical Engineering
and 12 years paper machine project engineering experience. I
have an excellent reputation for completing projects on time and
under budget. Some of my major achievements include:

- Completion of $49 million rebuild of twin wire former on
  time and under budget ($1.5 million savings)

- Lead wet end Project Engineer for purchase, design and
  installation of new $104 million Beloit paper machine
  (wet end savings of $920K)

- Senior Project Engineer for $29 million rebuild of drying
  section of twin wire tissue machine (project completed 2
  months ahead of schedule with $65K savings)

Although knowledgeable of most machine configurations, I am
particularly experienced with twin wire formers and some of the
newer state-of-the-art sheet forming technology. This should
prove very additive to companies engaged in upgrading their
papermaking technology.

My current compensation is $52,000, and I am looking for annual
compensation in the high-$50K range.

Should you be in the market for strong paper machine project
engineering talent, I would appreciate the opportunity to
further discuss my qualifications with you. I can be reached at
(414) 952-1725.

Thank you.

Sincerely yours,

*Scott M. Beatty*

Scott Michael Beatty

gth

Enclosure

SAMPLE F *General Broadcast Letter*

125 Sheering Place
Blue Lake, VA 19732
February 6, 1992

Ms Sharon W. Reeder
Vice President of Human Resources
The Childon Company
155 Rock Ridge Road
Memphis, TN 19372

Dear Ms Reeder:

Please accept the enclosed resume as my application for a
position with The Childon Company as Director of Corporate
Employment. Should you have an appropriate opening at this
level, I feel you will likely find my credentials to be of
interest.

My background includes an M.S. degree in Industrial Relations
from Michigan State University coupled with 14 years experience
in Human Resources. This includes nearly 9 years in the
employment function - 6 years as Manager of Administrative
Employment for General Electronics, Inc., and nearly 3 years as
a National Practice Director for Russell J. Reynolds, a major
international executive search consulting firm.

I have managed a Fortune 200 employment function and have
recruited executive, managerial and professional employees for a
wide range of industries and functional areas. I have earned a
reputation for cost effective, timely and high quality
employment and am thoroughly trained in behavioral-based
interviewing and evaluation techniques.

If you are seeking a knowledgeable, skilled Director for your
Corporate Employment function, may I suggest we meet to further
discuss my qualifications and the contributions that I might
make to The Childon Company.

Thank you for your consideration.

Sincerely,

*Bruce A. Langstrom*

Bruce A. Langstrom

rad

Enclosure

122 Oyster Road
Kingston, RI 17364
May 23, 1992

Mr. Raymond D. Barker
Manager of Corporate Accounting
Blakesmith Company, Inc.
112 Fruend Road
Lancaster, PA 19847

Dear Mr. Barker:

I am writing to apply for the position of Cost Accountant in
your Corporate Accounting function. I feel that I have excellent
qualifications for this position, and would appreciate your
consideration of the enclosed resume.

I hold a B.S. degree in Accounting from Villanova University and
have over ten years of employment in the Accounting profession.
This includes some 6 years as an Auditor with Price Waterhouse
and another four years as a Cost Accountant with the Redding
Company. During this time I received excellent training and
experience. Additionally, as copies of past performance
evaluations will attest, I have consistently sustained excellent
performance.

My current earnings are $42,000 per year, and I would expect
some reasonable improvement over this amount.

Although open to relocation, my preference is for the Mid
Atlantic States. Other locations will be considered depending
upon the specifics of the opportunity.

If you feel that your Corporate Accounting function could
benefit from the contributions of a seasoned, knowledgeable Cost
Accountant, I would appreciate hearing from you. I can be
reached during normal business hours at (215) 472-9586.

Thank you for your consideration, and I look forward to hearing
from you.

Sincerely,

Blake R. Remington

Blake R. Remington

erm

Enclosure

115 Baylor Road
Springfield Ma 87375
October 19, 1995

Ms Barbara A. Cunningham
Chief Financial Officer
The R. J. Elliott Company, Inc.
999 Franklin Street
Boston, MA 73291

Dear Ms Cunningham:

Should you be in the market for a seasoned, accomplished Senior
Financial Analyst who has established an excellent reputation
for successful acquisition analysis, the enclosed resume should
be of interest to you.

My background includes an M.B.A. in Finance from the Wharton
School coupled with over 6 years experience in acquisition
analysis with the Corporate Business Development Department of a
Fortune 100 consumer products company. During this time I
completed analysis of 26 potential acquisition targets, which
resulted in successful acquisition of 6 highly successful
companies. These included:

- a $30 million acquisition of a baking company that has
  provided a 22% average ROI for the first two years of
  operation

- a $22 million acquisition of a foods distribution company
  showing an 18% ROI in the third year of operation

- a $55 million purchase of a plastic wrap manufacturer
  that has yielded a 11% return during the first full
  year of operation

Importantly, all companies acquired have been profitable, with
the lowest ROI standing at 6.2%. Additionally, all acquisitions
where successfully concluded at an average purchase price of 2.3
times net profit.

I would welcome the opportunity to meet with you to discuss how,
as a Senior Analyst, I might make similar contributions to your
firm. Should you wish to explore this matter in greater detail,
please contact me at (212) 485-2957.

Thank you. I appreciate your consideration.

Sincerely,

Janet A. Morse

Janet A. Morse

sam

Enclosure

SAMPLE I *General Broadcast Letter*

825 Lincoln Highway
Phoenix, AZ 17493
December 15, 1989

Mr. Samuel Fathing
Vice President of Logistics
North American Corporation
325 North Wilcox Street
Chicago, IL 18274

Dear Mr. Fathing:

As the senior Logistics executive of a leading consumer foods
company, you may be in need of a top flight Purchasing Manager
who can make immediate contributions to the profitability of
your operations.

As the Senior Purchasing Agent for a Fortune 300, $1.2 billion
consumer food products company, I have enjoyed a reputation as a
tough but fair negotiator who has made significant cost savings
contributions to my employer. These contributions have included:

- saved $36 million per year through computerization of the
  raw materials tracking and forecasting process

- saved $22 million through corporate-wide consolidation of
  packaging supplies purchases

- realized $18 million annual savings through conversion to
  biomass fuels with long-term purchase contract

- negotiated 3-year shipping carton contract worth $6
  million in annual cost savings

My credentials include a B.S. degree in Packaging Engineering
and an M.B.A. in Finance. Additionally, I have over 13 years of
purchasing experience with a major international corporation.

My salary requirements are in the low $60K range, and I am
completely open to relocation.

Should you feel that I can contribute to your purchasing
function in a corporate management capacity, I would welcome the
opportunity for a personal interview with you and the members of
your staff. I can be reached at (316) 978-1739.

I appreciate your consideration.

Sincerely,

*Karen B. Robinson*

Karen B. Robinson

kbr

Enclosure

265 West Rampart Street
Atlanta, GA 19739
March 22, 1993

Ms Katherine A. Carter
Vice President of Logistics
Bellweather Corporation
635 East River Road
Wilmington, DL 10385

Dear Ms Carter:

I am writing to express my interest in a position as Manager of
Procurement with Bellweather Corporation. As a leader in the
field of consumer paper products, I felt that you may well have
an interest in a professional with extensive procurement
background in the purchase of corrugated, flexible packaging and
cardboard cartons.

As the enclosed resume will attest, I have over 15 years
experience in procurement with a Fortune 200 manufacturer of
consumer products, where I managed an annual materials
procurement budget of $250 million. Specific contributions
included:

- Saved $1.3 million through negotiation of 2-year contract
  to purchase knockdowns at 20% below current price.

- Realized annual savings of $575K through inventory
  reductions resulting from tighter control through
  computer forecasting.

- Saved $200 thousand annually through renegotiation of
  poly wrap contract at 10% reduction in purchase price.

Should you be in need of a knowledgeable, seasoned procurement
manager who can make similar contributions to your firm's bottom
line, please contact me at (214) 758-2958. I would welcome the
opportunity to meet with you personally.

Thank you for your consideration, and I look forward to hearing
from you.

Sincerely yours,

*Christopher Todd Beatty*

Christopher Todd Beatty

gth

Enclosure

# 8

# EXECUTIVE SEARCH
# COVER LETTERS

The cover letter used to transmit your résumé to an executive search firm, although a type of broadcast letter, differs from the general broadcast letter used to correspond with employers. This difference has to do with the needs of these two organizations. Let's take a few moments to examine these needs.

The employer's motivation when reading a cover letter and attached résumé is to hire someone who will be value adding to the corporation. In this regard, he or she is looking for evidence that the candidate has the ability to solve certain key problems, apply new methods and technology, and generally assist in the attainment of the organization's strategic goals and mission.

If the employer has done the necessary homework, the basic knowledge, skills, and capabilities needed to successfully perform the key functions of the job have been identified. The employer then translates these factors into selection criteria against which prospective candidates will be measured.

Additionally, if proper care is taken to select persons who will be both successful and happy in the organization, the employer must also attempt to determine how compatible job candidates will be with the culture of the organization. To do this properly, the employer must define certain personal traits and characteristics, philosophy, and style that will best fit the organization's culture. These factors are added to the list of previously determined technical qualifications to arrive at candidate selection criteria.

When formulating selection criteria, forward-thinking companies also consider another dimension, which has to do with the strategic changes that the organization will need to make if it is to be successful in realizing its longer-term strategic objectives. The employer then translates these changes into new knowledge and skill requirements necessary to drive the required changes needed to realize these goals.

The final result of this in-depth analysis of the current job, organizational culture, and strategic needs of the organization is a list of specific selection criteria against which employment candidates will be measured during the interview and employment selection process.

Although an executive search firm may participate to some degree in defining these selection criteria, most of them have already been fairly well-defined by the employer prior to the search firm's arrival on the scene. Thus the executive search firm does not normally have an in-depth understanding of the hiring organization's requirements. Instead, in most cases, it simply discusses the selection criteria with the employer to make sure they are understood, and then sets off to find the candidate who best meets them.

In short, the employer is looking for someone who will be value adding, while the search firm is looking for someone who best matches the selection criteria. The search firm therefore has a more narrow perspective than does the employer, who has the benefit of knowing all of the various intricacies and special internal needs of his or her organization and thus reads the cover letter looking for evidence that the candidate will be value adding. The search firm, on the other hand, typically views it as a simple letter of transmittal, and moves quickly to the résumé to make a comparison between the candidate's qualifications and the selection criteria.

The cover letter is far less likely to make a sale to the executive search firm than it is to the employer. This fact suggests, then, that the cover letters used to transmit your résumé to these two organizations need to be handled differently.

## Letter Elements

The basic elements of the executive search cover letter are as follows:

1. Return address
2. Date
3. Search firm address
4. Salutation
5. Introductory paragraph or statement
6. Statement of job objective
7. Brief summary of qualifications
8. Value-adding statement (optional)
9. Reason for making change (optional)
10. Salary requirements (optional)
11. Geographical preferences/restrictions (optional)
12. Statement of willingness to provide additional information
13. Instructions for reaching you
14. Statement of appreciation
15. Complimentary close
16. Signature

## Introductory Paragraph

The introductory paragraph usually accomplishes two things. First, it acknowledges the role of the executive search firm in helping client organizations find key professionals and executives. Second, it states your job objective.

Here are some very typical introductory paragraphs:

*I am currently seeking a senior-level position in manufacturing management. Perhaps one of your current search assignments requires such an individual.*

*I am a seasoned financial executive with Fortune 100 experience. Please consider the enclosed résumé in light of your current assignments for top financial management talent.*

*I have decided to make a career change and am currently seeking a position as a CEO or COO. Please consider my background for any appropriate active or future executive search assignments requiring someone with my credentials.*

As you can see, the statement of job objective is usually included in the opening paragraph along with the request to be considered as a candidate for current or future assignments.

Read the sample cover letters at the end of this chapter for some additional ideas on how to structure your lead-in paragraph.

## Qualifications Summary

The executive search cover letter normally contains a paragraph that briefly summarizes the candidate's overall qualifications. This includes educational credentials as well as professional work experience.

When summarizing work experience, it is important to cite only what is supportive of your stated job objective. Don't bore the reader by including nonrelated assignments. Also, be brief. Stick to only the basic information needed to crystalize your qualifications, and don't drone on and on with the details of your background. If well-written, your résumé will accomplish all of this.

The following are some sample qualification summaries. Additional examples are found at the end of this chapter.

*I hold an M.B.A. in Marketing from the University of Chicago and a B.S. in Mechanical Engineering from the University of Michigan. My background includes nearly eighteen years in marketing and sales management, with the last five years as Director of Marketing for the Cranston Corporation, a Fortune 200 manufacturer of fastening devices.*

*A graduate of the University of Delaware with an M.S. in Chemical Engineering, I have been employed in the Central Research Group of the DuPont Company for the last nine years, where I have become thoroughly versed in synthetic fiber development. My creativity as a Research Scientist is supported by eight current patents with an additional six pending.*

*I am a seasoned project engineer with over twelve years experience in paper machine project engineering. I have successfully managed paper machine capital projects valued at over $80 million. My professional credentials include an M.S. in Mechanical Engineering and a Professional Engineer license from the Commonwealth of Pennsylvania.*

### Value-Adding Statement (Optional)

A value-adding statement is intended to convey your ability to make meaningful contributions to the search firm's client organization. As indicated, although important to the general broadcast cover letter, it is considered optional in the executive search cover letter. If cleverly written, this statement can have a positive impact on the reader, but for the most part, it is considered to have little impact on the decision of the executive search firm, where the focus is on matching qualifications with the client organization's requirements, not on value adding. The search firm's main focus is thus on the résumé rather than on the cover letter that introduces it.

The value-adding statement(s) usually consists of major job-related accomplishments. These are carefully tailored to the anticipated needs of the employer and normally fall into one or more of the following categories:

1. Related to the ongoing functional objectives of the job
2. Related to the strategic goals of the hiring organization
3. The ability to apply new methods and state-of-the-art technology

The following are some examples of value-adding statements for your review. Certain of the sample cover letters at the end of this chapter also contain such statements.

*The following key accomplishments as a manufacturing executive should provide evidence of my ability to make meaningful contributions to one of your client organizations:*

- *Restructured manufacturing organization resulting in 20% headcount reduction and annual savings of $3 million.*
- *Installed Deming-based total quality program accounting for 22% scrap reduction ($1.2 million annual savings) and 80% reduction in customer complaints.*
- *Instituted JIT methods for control of raw materials inventory—$1 million annual savings.*

*As a seasoned project engineering manager, I can make significant contributions to one of your clients. Consider the following achievements:*

- *Successfully managed $20 million capital expansion of Templeton Mill—completed on time and 10% under budget.*
- *Installed TDC 2000 control system in the converting department of Wilmington Plant—annual savings of $2 million.*
- *Developed, designed, and installed new web forming device, increasing machine speeds by 18%—annual savings of $1.7 million.*

*My résumé will attest that, as an internal Organization Effectiveness Consultant, I have consistently provided state-of-the-art leadership in applying the most recent thinking to major program development. Perhaps I can make similar contributions to one of your clients. Please consider the following accomplishments:*

- *Transitioned major manufacturing organization from traditional departmental structure to customer-focused, product stream organization concept.*
- *Worked with Senior Vice President to successfully transition key division from traditional management philosophy to participatory management-based systems.*
- *Trained over 200 middle and senior management in the use of facilitator skills and management process design concepts.*

In each of the above examples, you will note that the author utilizes language that encourages the executive search firm to make the connection between the accomplishments cited and the value that could be derived through your employment by one of the firm's clients.

### Reason for Making Change (Optional)

As indicated, providing the search firm with a specific reason for wanting to make a change is optional. From an initial screening standpoint, it seldom adds to cover letter effectiveness and may, in fact, be detrimental to your employment campaign depending upon circumstances.

This subject was discussed in detail in Chapter 6, "Cover Letter Inclusions/Exclusions." Rather than be redundant, I suggest you consult this chapter for the guidelines that I have provided. For the most part, however, explaining your reasons for change is unnecessary and adds little to the effectiveness of the executive search cover letter.

### Salary Requirements (Optional)

Generally, the inclusion of salary requirements is considered optional in the executive search cover letter. It is usually to your benefit, however, to exclude such information. In this way, you assure yourself of maximum flexibility and control by not automatically screening yourself from consideration on the basis of income requirements that are considered too high for a given opportunity. Nevertheless, there are times when you may want to include your compensation requirements in the letter. This is particularly true when you are currently employed and unwilling to consider a lower compensation level, regardless of the opportunity.

If you elect to include your salary requirements in the cover letter, however, remember that there is always the unusual opportunity that, regardless of short-term income reduction, may offer significant future advancement and corresponding income growth potential considerably beyond that of your current position.

### Geographical Preferences/Restrictions (Optional)

As with salary requirements, inclusion of a statement concerning geographical preferences or restrictions may be somewhat limiting, and might serve to screen you out from a career opportunity that you might otherwise deem very desirable. Why take this chance?

It is felt that inclusion of geographical factors does little to enhance the overall effectiveness of executive search cover letters and, in most cases, can actually prove detrimental. Remember, if the executive search firm approaches you about a particular opportunity with one of its clients, you can always decline the chance to pursue it should geographical factors not be to your liking.

By being open to geographical considerations, you at least allow yourself the chance to weigh this factor against other, perhaps more important criteria, such as future growth and potential. If the opportunity for advancement is unusually good, you may just decide to waive geographical considerations. By excluding them from the cover letter, you at least preserve your options rather than prematurely foreclose on what might be an excellent job opportunity. The decision, of course, is up to you.

You may now wish to review the following sample letters for some ideas on structuring your own. I hope you will find them very helpful.

125 First Avenue
Dallas, TX 39874
October 21, 1989

Mr. David Branston
Senior Partner
Branston & McClain
1524 West Patterson Street
San Francisco, CA 19746

Dear Mr. Branston:

Could one of your clients in the San Francisco area use a successful and experienced engineering executive or program manager?

My broad experience in the engineering and manufacturing areas of computer equipment and office automation, coupled with my expertise in managing the introduction of new products, could be of interest to one of your client companies.

My credentials include a M.S. degree in Electrical Engineering coupled with over fifteen years experience in the development and engineering of computer and related electronic equipment. This includes six years as Research Manager of Dynatech, a $300 million manufacturer of printed circuit boards.

Although my compensation level is not as important to me as finding the right opportunity, you may wish to be aware that my total compensation package has ranged between $65,000 and $75,000 over the last few years.

If my experience and background fit the requirements for one of your searches, please contact me during the day at (912) 473-8952 or at home at (912) 476-3857.

Thank you for your consideration.

Sincerely,

*Linda D. Baker*

Linda D. Baker

mar

Enclosure

**SAMPLE B** *Executive Search Cover Letter*

116 North Covington Lane
Richmond, VA 74893
September 19, 1996

Ms Roberta C. Phillips
Lane, Smith & Lantrop
235 East Market Street
Sunnydale, MI 29837

Dear Ms Phillips:

I am writing to you because I am seeking new opportunities for career advancement in the field of Training and Development. Perhaps one of your current clients may have some interest in my background.

My credentials include a Doctorate degree and eight years of experience in the field, during which I have been involved in the full complement of Human Resource Development operations and have progressed from trainer to management level. Currently I am serving as a part-time evening faculty member of the Masters degree program in Training and Development at Michigan State University. I am also doing some part-time consulting in Organization Development.

Although I would prefer to live in the Michigan area, I would be open to other geographical areas for the right career opportunity.

Should you be aware of a suitable opportunity with one of your client organizations, I would appreciate hearing from you. I can be reached on a confidential basis during the day at (316) 739-3846.

Thank you.

Sincerely,

*John B. Lindsay*

John B. Lindsay

dgr

Enclosure

116 East Main Street
Clinton, OH 28375
October 26, 1992

Mr. Arthur Lansome
Senior Partner
Lansome, Voltaire & Smith
Executive Search Consultants
26 Ivory Tower Suites
1000 Capital Parkway
Cleveland, OH 29883

Dear Mr. Lansome:

Enclosed please find my resume for your review against any of
your client's requirements for a corporate or divisional
Controller. In the event you do not currently have an active
assignment that is appropriate, I would appreciate your retaining
my file for review against future search assignments in the
financial field.

I hold an M.B.A. in Finance from the Wharton Business School and
have over 15 years financial and accounting experience in
positions of increasing accountability. Currently, I am the
Corporate Controller of Utex Corporation, a $390 million
manufacturer of spraying equipment, where I report directly to
the President and manage a staff of 32 employees.

Growth opportunities at Utex are limited, and I have made the
decision to move on with my career. I am interested in a position
as C.F.O. for a medium-sized company, but would consider a
division-level assignment as a Controller for a major company. I
would also consider positions in financial consulting.

My current compensation level is $105K, including bonus. I would
consider appropriate opportunities at or above this level. At
this stage of my career, potential future growth is a more
important consideration than immediate income.

Should one of your clients be in the market for someone with my
skills in the financial area, I would appreciate hearing from
you. If necessary, I can be reached at my office during the day,
on a confidential basis. My office number is (416) 677-5533.

Thank you for your consideration.

Sincerely,

*Walter B. Peters*

Walter B. Peters

rsm

Enclosure

**SAMPLE D** *Executive Search Cover Letter*


126 East Hanover Street
Wellsville, TX 88736
January 22, 1994


Ms Katherine Weller
Vice President
Fuller, Klinger & Schmidt
109 East Commerce Drive
Dallas, TX 87392


Dear Ms Weller:

I am seeking a senior-level position in Operations management.
Perhaps one of your current or future clients may have an
interest in my capabilities.

I hold an M.S. degree in Industrial Management from Ohio State
University and have over 16 years of experience in Operations,
with 8 years in management. As Director of Manufacturing for
Belcher Corporation, a $185 million manufacturer of specialty
pumps for the chemical industry, I managed a staff of 25
professionals and directed all manufacturing operations for 6
separate manufacturing sites.

In my current position, I am credited with annual savings of
nearly $18 million as the result of innovative programs
introduced during the last four years. These include statistical
process control, Just-in-Time management, and product stream
management. I pride myself on staying current in all major new
developments in the field of Operations, and am frequently one of
the first to try them.

If one of your clients seeks a highly-motivated Operations
executive who has a demonstrated record of substantial cost
reduction and productivity improvement, perhaps you will think of
me.

Should you wish to contact me during the day, I can be reached at
(416) 977-3974 on a confidential basis.

Thank you for your consideration.

Sincerely,

*Carlos B. Schwartz*

Carlos B. Schwartz


dmr

Enclosure

## SAMPLE E *Executive Search Cover Letter*

132 Mifflin Road
Mifflinville, WA 38975
July 16, 1991

Mr. Richard S. Brabson
Senior Vice President
Banard, Simpson & Lee
Consultants in Executive Search
123 Wayland Blvd.
Seattle, WA 38726

Dear Mr. Brabson:

It has come to my attention that your firm has some specialization in executive search in the Materials-related fields. Since I am seeking a senior-level position in the Purchasing field, it seems appropriate that I forward my resume to your attention for review against current executive search consulting assignments in this field.

As you can see from the enclosed resume, I have an M.B.A. from the University of Washington, with a major in Industrial Management, and a B.S. degree in Industrial Engineering from the same school. My professional experience includes over 20 years in Materials-related areas, including over 10 years in Purchasing management.

The enclosed resume will attest to the fact that I have established an excellent track record in bringing about major cost reduction and overall efficiency improvement to the Purchasing functions of past employers. I am particularly skillful at negotiating long-term vital supply contracts for bulk purchase of raw materials and vital supplies and, at the same time, realizing substantial reduction in capital investment in inventories through application of Just-in-Time concepts. Perhaps I could make similar contributions to one of your valued clients.

My compensation requirements are in the $70K to $80K range, and I am open to relocation with the exception of East Coast metropolitan areas.

Should you require further information, I can be reached during business hours (on a confidential basis) at (206) 977-1395.

Thank you.

Sincerely,

Barbara S. Smartz
Barbara S. Smartz

asm

Enclosure

**SAMPLE F** *Executive Search Cover Letter*

201 West Ocean Court
Tampa, FL 87391
May 24, 1990

Ms Judith A. Walker
Senior Principal
Walker, Kelly & Smith
100 Merritt Road, SW
Atlanta, GA 16395

Dear Ms Walker:

Perhaps one of your current search assignments calls for a
seasoned Director of Research in specialty chemicals or related
fields. If so, you may find my credentials quite interesting.

A Ph.D. in Organic Chemistry from Georgia Institute of
Technology, I have over 18 years in specialty chemicals research
and development, both as a professional and as a manager.
Currently, I am Director of Research for Baxter Chemicals, a $350
million manufacturer of specialty chemicals sold to the Pulp &
Paper Industry. In this capacity, I report to the President and
manage a 80-person research staff involved with advanced research
and applications development of paper machine wet end chemical
specialties.

As my enclosed resume will attest, I have made significant
contributions to my current employer. Namely, in the last 5 years
as Research Director, I have led development and successful
introduction of over 30 new products. These have accounted for an
overall increase in sales from $110 million to $350 million for
Baxter Chemicals, a significant milestone by most standards.
Perhaps one of your clients may have interest in duplicating this
achievement and significantly increasing revenues through
innovative product development.

I am completely open on the subject of relocation, and would
consider opportunities anywhere in the U.S. I would also be
receptive to discussing overseas assignments.

Should you wish to contact me, I can be reached during the day at
(212) 875-1234.

Thank you for your consideration, and I look forward to the
prospect of hearing from you about an appropriate career
opportunity with one of your client organizations.

Sincerely,

*David R. Grace*

David R. Grace

cmd

Enclosure

# 9

## ADVERTISING RESPONSE COVER LETTERS

$E$mployment advertising, whether in the local newspaper or in a specialty publication, has long been an important resource for experienced employment professionals seeking to fill positions within their companies. This does not mean that, although frequently used, such advertising is particularly effective. In fact, knowledgeable employment sources estimate that only between 10 and 14 percent of all jobs filled in the United States are filled as a result of advertising. This compares with an estimated 70 percent filled through personal contact and employment networking. Nonetheless, advertisements are considered an important source in job hunting and should therefore be a part of your job search campaign.

It is important to be aware that employment advertising can be found in a wide variety of publications. The most common is the classified section of the newspaper. There are, however, several other publications that should be regularly checked for job opportunities. These include speciality newspapers (i.e., *The National Business Employment Weekly* and *The National Ad Search*), professional association newsletters, trade association publications, and specialty publications related to specific professions and industries (i.e., trade journals and periodicals).

Employers long ago learned that specialty publications can be a particularly productive source for employment advertising. This is because they are targeted toward a very specific audience. For example, when searching for technical professionals, many employers in the pulp and paper industry will frequently advertise in the *Tappi Journal*, a monthly periodical published by the Technical Association of the Pulp and Paper Industry and mailed to thousands of industry technical and manufacturing professionals. Similar specialized publications exist for many professions and industries. A little research at your local library will help you to identify them. A call to your professional or industry association can also prove helpful in acquiring this information.

### Some Differences

The cover letter used to respond to employment advertising is different from the general broadcast letter sent to employers or executive search firms. In particular, it is more targeted and focused, and is specifically directed to the requirements of the employer as set forth in the advertisement.

Actually, employment candidates have a decided advantage when designing a cover letter that responds to recruitment advertising. Unlike the general mailing campaign, where the candidate must do considerable industry research to define the employer's probable needs, the advertisement usually spells out these requirements in specific detail. This allows the applicant to design a highly targeted response that focuses on these specific requirements, and thus measurably increases the opportunity for generating a favorable response from the employer.

Given this opportunity, however, it never ceases to amaze me how many applicants fail to take full advantage of it and continue to respond to such advertisements using a general broadcast letter that fails to address the real needs of the employer. Such general responses will normally fall short in addressing the specific requirements of the advertised position, leaving the employer to guess whether you have the qualifications desired. They can also suggest that your interest level is not sufficiently high for you to prepare an appropriate cover letter, or, worse yet, that you are simply too lazy to do so. Neither impression will aid your cause.

In many cases, you could be one of several hundred people who are responding to the ad. If, under these circumstances, you fail to tailor an appropriate cover letter that addresses specific requirements, you are placing yourself at a decided disadvantage compared to those who do. Rather than highlighting those qualifications sought by the prospective employer and thereby increasing your chances of selection, you are relying on the employer to ferret out this information from the résumé. In such cases, the employer may well decide to forgo your employment candidacy in favor of someone whose qualifications for the position are clearly highlighted in the cover letter.

Why leave this matter to chance? If you are truly interested in the advertised position, it is strongly recommended that you take the time to carefully design an effective cover letter. By doing so, you substantially improve your chances of getting an employment interview.

## Advertisement Analysis

The first step in designing an effective response to an employment advertisement is to study the ad to determine position requirements. The next step is to analyze your qualifications to determine which of the employer's requirements they meet. The cover letter will then be designed in such a way as to focus the reader's attention on the similarities between your specific qualifications and the stated requirements of the position—a comparison most employers will appreciate.

In order to facilitate the advertisement analysis process, I have provided the following set of questions that should prove helpful in getting the information you will need to prepare an effective cover letter and maximize your marketability.

1. What are the educational qualifications required for the position (i.e., degree level and major). Describe below:

_____

_____

_____

2. What are your educational qualifications (i.e., degree level and major). Describe below:

_____

_____

_____

3. What, if any, special skills training is required or preferred (beyond formal education)? Describe below:

_____

_____

_____

4. Have you had such special skills training? If so, describe the skill and the training you received.

_____

_____

_____

5. What technical or scientific knowledge does the position require (e.g., surface chemistry, statistical process control, salary surveys, Just-in-Time manufacturing, etc.)? List below:

_____

_____

_____

_____

_____

_____

6. In which of these areas are you knowledgeable? What evidence can you cite of your proficiency? Describe:

_____

_____

_____

_____

_____

7. If a managerial position, what is the scope of experience required (functions managed, number of employees, budgets, etc.)? Describe below:

_____

_____

_____

_____

_____

_____

_____

8. Which of these managerial experience requirements do you satisfy?
   Describe below:

_____

_____

_____

_____

_____

_____

_____

9. How many years of experience are required, and at what level? (By
   "level" I mean professional versus managerial level.) Describe:

_____

_____

_____

10. How many years of experience do you have at these levels? Indicate
    below:

_____

_____

11. What specific personal traits and characteristics are sought? List below:

_____

_____

_____

_____

12. Which of these personal traits and characteristics do you possess? Cite below:

_____

_____

_____

_____

This analysis will equip you to make a direct comparison between the specific requirements of the employer, as stated in the ad, and your own qualifications. This comparative information is then used as the basis for your cover letter construction and ensures that this information will be readily available when needed.

## Special Emphasis

Review of the specific wording chosen by the employer in an advertisement can often yield some tangible clues about qualifications that are of particular interest to that employer. Most ads are slanted to emphasize the need for a particular strength in a given area. Careful reading of the ad copy may reveal what that area is.

Be alert for key words and phrases that are frequently used to convey special interest in a particular area of qualification. Examples of such key words and phrases are:

Required
Is required
Must be
Must have
Must be capable of
Desirable
Very desirable
Must be thoroughly versed in/knowledgeable of
Should be strong in

In addition to these special words or phrases, you should also be particularly alert for any repetition in the ad. If a specific qualification is repeated, you can bet the ranch that this is an area of particular interest to the employer. Such repetition usually means that the author of the advertisement wanted to make sure that this particular point was well covered, which, in turn, usually means that this is an area that will take on strong significance in the candidate selection process.

If you are able to discover a particular area of emphasis in the ad, be sure to take full advantage of it. If you have particularly strong qualifications in this special interest area, consider including in your cover letter a brief, separate paragraph that highlights those qualifications. If you are qualified in other areas specified as well, such a paragraph could well serve as a key factor in winning a personal interview.

## Letter Components

Review of the sample cover letters at the end of this chapter will reveal that the advertising response cover letter contains certain standard components. These are, of course, in addition to the normal return address, date line, employer's address, and salutation. These components are as follows:

1.  Reference to advertisement
2.  Expression of interest in position
3.  Comparison of position requirements with personal qualifications
4.  Statement of additional qualifications (optional)

   5.  Salary requirements statement (optional)
   6.  Geographical preference statement (optional)
   7.  Contact information
   8.  Request for response or interview
   9.  Statement of appreciation

   You will note that certain of these components are considered optional and may be either included in or excluded from the letter depending upon how each adds or detracts from your overall candidacy. If you are adamant about compensation requirements or geographical considerations, then, by all means, include these items. Realize, however, that, as previously discussed, such inclusion will almost definitely have an adverse effect on your candidacy and, in certain circumstances, will cause you to be screened out from further employment consideration. Perhaps you may be better off excluding these items and reserving final judgment on compensation or location until after you have had the opportunity to consider the specifics of a given opportunity. The choice is yours.

   The introductory paragraphs of the sample letters at the end of this chapter will reveal a specific mention of the position advertisement. Included in this reference are the name of the publication in which the ad appeared, the date of publication, and the position title, so that there is no confusion about the position for which you are applying. It should be pointed out that large companies, in particular, may be running simultaneous ads for numerous positions. Additionally, the advertisement response may, in some cases, be referred to different members of the employment function for review. If there is confusion in your letter as to the position, your letter and résumé could well end up being reviewed by someone unfamiliar with the specifics of the position for which you are applying, which could prove fatal to your inquiry.

   You will see that each of the sample cover letters at the end of this chapter also includes a specific statement of interest in the position for which the applicant is applying. Such interest statements should convey a sense of excitement and enthusiasm about the opening, which does not go unnoticed by the prospective employers and may serve to set your response apart from the hundreds of others they are likely to receive. In this regard, a little enthusiasm can go a long way toward creating interest in your candidacy.

   Another standard feature of the advertising response cover letter is the comparison of your qualifications with the requirements stated in the ad. As the sample cover letters will attest, this comparison can use either a linear (line comparison) or a literary (paragraph comparison) approach. Either way, if done effectively, it can be a very powerful tool in leading the employer to the conclusion that you are well qualified for the position and deserving of an interview. It is clearly the key factor in designing an effective advertising response cover letter and thus deserves special attention.

The remaining components of the advertising response cover letter (i.e., contact information, request for response or interview, and statement of appreciation) have already been fully discussed in previous chapters and will not be discussed here.

### The Linear Comparison

When using the linear comparison, the general approach is to begin by stating your belief that you are qualified for the position. This statement is then followed by line-by-line delineation of your qualifications that directly relate to the specific requirements contained in the advertisement. The following are some examples of the linear comparison technique:

Example A

*Careful review of your requirements suggests that I am well qualified for the position of Materials Control Manager. Please consider the following:*

1.  *M.B.A. degree with materials management emphasis*
2.  *10 years materials flow experience*
3.  *3 years materials control management with Fortune 200 company*
4.  *thoroughly trained in JIT applications*
5.  *heavily experienced in "total quality" vendor qualification methods*
6.  *8 years experience in the consumer products industry*

Example B

*My credentials would appear to be an exact fit for the position of Director of Corporate Employment, as described in your advertisement. Please consider the following:*

1.  *M.B.A. from Cornell University*
2.  *B.S. degree in Industrial Management*
3.  *20 years Fortune 500 employment experience, 8 in corporate employment*

4. *6 years employment management experience*
5. *senior level management recruitment experience*
6. *extensive use of executive search firms*
7. *management of high-volume technical recruitment in electronics industry*

In each example, the factors listed in the linear comparison address a specific requirement listed by the employer in the advertisement. Further examples of the linear comparison are contained in the sample cover letters at the end of this chapter.

Generally, I recommend the linear comparison over the literary comparison, particularly when the employment applicant has most or all of the qualifications called for in the ad. This line-by-line description of qualifications is easily read, and the reader may find it less offensive than the literary comparison since, unlike the literary comparison, there is no repetition of what is contained in the employment advertisement.

Let's now take a look at the literary comparison approach.

### The Literary Comparison

The literary approach is recommended when only some of the employer's requirements are met. In such cases, use of the linear comparison will tend to make it too easy for the employer to spot the missing qualifications. Under these circumstances, the literary approach will better suit your purposes.

When using the literary comparison, you repeat a portion of the advertisement in the cover letter and then follow with a short description of your related qualifications. This approach facilitates comparison with requirements set forth in the recruitment ad and serves to highlight your qualifications to fill the position.

The following are some examples of the literary comparison approach:

Example A

*Your ad states that you are seeking a "Ph.D. statistician with over 10 years of experience in the field of total quality." I hold a Ph.D. in Statistics from Washington University and have been employed by Radnor Corporation in the field of total quality for the last 12 years. Currently, I am the Manager of Total Quality for the corporation.*

Example B

*According to your ad, you are seeking a "Senior Project Engineer with a degree in Mechanical Engineering and over 8 years experience in paper machine project engineering."*

*I have an M.S. in Mechanical Engineering from the University of Michigan, and have been employed in the capacity of paper machine project engineer with Deltar Paper Company since 1977. During this time, I have played a primary role in the installation and/or rebuild of 6 paper machines. My last project entailed a $23 million rebuild of a light weight coated paper machine to include state-of-the-art, on-line coating technology.*

The balance of this chapter contains several examples of employment advertisements, along with sample responses. You will note how these letters employ the comparison techniques just discussed, along with the other letter components discussed earlier.

Careful study of these letters and the recommendations made in this chapter should enable you to construct good cover letters that effectively respond to employment advertising and that enhance the probability of employment interviews.

# DIRECTOR OF TOTAL QUALITY

Fortune 200 leader in the manufacture of printing and converting grades of paper seeks Director of Total Quality for its Chicago-based corporate headquarters.

This position reports to the President and is responsible for providing leadership, as an inhouse consulting resource, to the President's staff, five operating locations and the field sales organization in the development of quality and productivity improvement processes, using statistical methodology as the basis. Will be responsible for the development and implementation of a corporate-wide Deming-based total quality program.

Position requires an advanced degree in Statistics and thorough training in the total quality philosophy and methodology of Dr. W. Edwards Deming. The successful candidate will be well-versed in the practical application of statistical techniques (e.g., design of experiments, control charting, variance analysis, etc.) to the development and implementation of a total quality program.

Qualified candidates will have extensive experience in the design, delivery and management of a variety of training courses in statistical methods. The preferred candidate will have facilitated, designed and successfully implemented a statistically based total quality program in a significant organizational unit.

Excellent compensation and comprehensive benefits program are provided.

Interested persons send complete resume and salary requirements in confidence to:

Mr. David R. Baxter
Director of Corporate Employment
The Fairfax Paper Company
825 Commerce Blvd.
Chicago, IL 18736

An Equal Opportunity Employer

**SAMPLE A** *Advertisement Response*

116 Warren Drive
West Chester, PA 19382
January 16, 1991

Mr. David R. Baxter
Director of Corporate Employment
The Fairfax Paper Company
825 Commerce Blvd.
Chicago, IL 18736

Dear Mr. Baxter:

Enclosed please find my resume in response to your recent advertisement in the January 6th edition of the <u>Chicago Tribune</u> for a Director of Total Quality. This position sounds exciting, and I would welcome the opportunity to discuss it further with you.

As my resume will attest, I would appear to have excellent qualifications for this position as follow:

1. Ph.D. in Statistics from the University of Florida.
2. Graduate of the W. Edwards Deming Institute - 1986.
3. Designed and successfully implemented corporate-wide total quality program at Wesson Foods.
4. Well-versed in the application of statistics to total quality (i.e., design of experiments, control charting, variance analysis, etc.).
5. Trained over 6,000 hourly workers, operations managers and engineers in statistical quality techniques (a 12 course program).

Should you also agree that my background is a good match for your requirements, I would welcome the opportunity to meet with you to further explore this excellent opportunity. I feel confident that I can provide the kind of leadership that you are seeking for your company's total quality effort.

Salary requirements are in the $90K to $100K range with some flexibility for negotiation dependent upon details of the total offer package.

I can be reached during the day on a confidential basis at my office. My office phone number is (215) 784-2969.

Thank you for your consideration, and I look forward to hearing from you.

Sincerely,

*Barbara A Snyder*

Barbara A. Snyder

arn

Enclosure

# SENIOR PROJECT ENGINEER
# PAPER MACHINES

Bramson Paper Company, a leading forest products company, is seeking several project engineers to staff a major $1.2 billion capital project, the largest such project ever undertaken by the company. Engineers will have complete project responsibility including feasibility studies, equipment selection, design modification, installation, start-up and debugging. This is an exciting opportunity for engineers seeking major project experience and accountability.

This position requires a B.S. degree in Mechanical Engineering plus 5 or more years experience in paper machine project engineering. Experience with twin wire forming machines is required, with wet end experience highly desirable. Must have demonstrated ability to independently handle major project accountability and provide technical direction to junior engineers. Familiarity with TDC 3000 control systems is also desirable.

Excellent growth potential exists for advancement into engineering management, dependent upon contribution and potential.

This position provides for an excellent base salary plus profit sharing. A full range of benefits is also provided.

Qualified candidates should submit their resume, including salary requirements, to:

Ms Ann L. Johnson
Manager of Technical Employment
Bramson Paper Company
200 East River Street
Dansford, MA 89372

We are an Equal Opportunity Employer

**SAMPLE B** *Advertisement Response*

Apartment 305<br>
Westbrook Arms<br>
202 Wilson Avenue<br>
Detroit, MI 29847<br>
June 22, 1994

Ms Ann L. Johnson
Manager of Technical Employment
Bramson Paper Company
200 East River Street
Dansford, MA 89372

Dear Ms Johnson:

Your advertisement in the May 24th issue of <u>Paper News</u> for a Senior Project Engineer - Paper Machines has peaked my interest. This sounds like an exciting opportunity that is in keeping with my current career goals, and I have therefore enclosed my resume for your consideration. I think you should find my qualifications well-suited to your needs.

Your ad calls for a B.S. in Mechanical Engineering with over 5 years experience in paper machine project experience. You state that twin wire forming and wet end experience are also desirable. I have a B.S. in Mechanical Engineering from Michigan Technological University and 6 years project experience with Appleton Paper Company in paper machine engineering. I have experience with twin wire formers and have also engineered the complete forming section, including all wet end systems, for a 280" fine paper machine.

As called for in your ad, I have worked independently on major project assignments (up to $6 million) and have led project teams of up to three project engineers. I also have extensive control systems experience.

It would appear that I am well-qualified for the position of Senior Project Engineer, and I would welcome the opportunity to further discuss this position with you and the members of your Engineering Staff.

My compensation requirements are in the $70K range.

I can be reached, on a confidential basis, during the day at (315) 875-3152 or at my home in the evening at (315) 786-5542.

Thank you for your consideration, and I look forward to hearing from you shortly.

Sincerely,<br>
John T. Orlander<br>
John T. Orlander

rsm

Enclosure

# OPERATIONS MANAGER

Leading engineering firm in the asbestos abatement industry, with sales in the $200 million range, seeks talented Operations Manager. This position reports to the Vice President of Consulting Engineering and is responsible for direction of 120-employee asbestos consulting and removal operation.

Position requires an undergraduate degree in engineering with 10 or more years management experience in the engineering construction or related industries. Must have solid experience in construction estimating and management of subcontract operations related to commercial and industrial structures. Knowledge of asbestos abatement and/or hazardous waste disposal helpful, but not required.

Our firm is experiencing dynamic growth and offers excellent opportunities for future professional advancement.

Waste Disposal, Inc. offers a highly competitive compensation package along with an exceptional flexible benefits program. Full relocation assistance also provided.

Send resume and compensation requirements to:

Christopher Waters
Manager of Human Resources
Waste Disposal, Inc.
100 Lancaster Road
Wilmington, DE 17395

**SAMPLE C** *Advertisement Response*


100 Murdock Lane
East Falls, NY 49205
August 30, 1990


Mr. Christopher Waters
Manager of Human Resources
Waste Disposal, Inc.
100 Lancaster Road
Wilmington, DE 17395


Dear Mr. Waters:

I read your July 28th ad for an Operations Manager in the <u>New York Times</u> with a great deal of interest. This position has strong appeal to me, and I am therefore submitting my credentials for your review and consideration.

It would appear that my background and experience are an excellent match for your needs, as demonstrated by the following highlights:

1. B.S. degree in Civil Engineering from Drexel University
2. 15 years experience in engineering construction and consulting; 8 in construction management
3. Estimated and managed large commercial and industrial construction projects in heating, air conditioning and HVAC ($30-40 million range, 100-200 subcontract employees)
4. Knowledge of chemical hazardous waste disposal


I have been watching the explosive growth of the hazardous waste engineering consulting industry, and I am excited with the prospects of joining your firm. I hope that you will give my application favorable consideration, and that I will have the opportunity to meet with you personally.

My current compensation at The Bradford Company is $65,000 per year. I would require compensation in the $70,000 to $75,000 range.

Should you wish to contact me, I can be reached at (317) 997-1287 during the day, or (317) 557-9827 during evening hours.

Thank you for your consideration, and I look forward to hearing from you in the near future.

Sincerely,

Carolyn A. Beatty
Carolyn A. Beatty


trm


Enclosure

# HUMAN RESOURCES MANAGER

Fortune 100 consumer products company seeks manager for Corporate Human Resources function. Position reports to the Vice President of Human Resources with functional accountability for organization design, human resources planning, internal and external staffing, development, and compensation and benefits administration. This position manages a staff of 42 professionals and provides human resource services to a 1,300-employee corporate headquarters facility.

The successful candidate will have a Masters degree in Human Resources Management or related area and 15 plus years broad experience in Human Resources as a generalist. Must have managed a sizeable organization and played a key role in leading cultural change from a traditional management system to one based upon participatory management principles. Must be a skilled facilitator capable of using management process designs to lead senior staff members in the development of strategic change and new directions.

Position requires someone who believes in the principles of participatory management and manages through the team approach. He/she will firmly believe in the importance of employee involvement and participation as "stakeholders" in the strategic goals of the organization. Must be an open, warm, approachable individual who generates trust and confidence in others.

Highly competitive compensation package includes base salary plus performance bonus. Outstanding benefits package also provided.

Qualified individuals should submit complete resume, including salary requirements and references, to:

Sandra F. Jenkins
Vice President of Human Resources
Bellstar Corporation
126 East 32nd Street
San Francisco, CA 64892

818 Thorton Lane
Waters Beach, CA 29845
May 20, 1991

Ms Sandra F. Jenkins
Vice President of Human Resources
Bellstar Corporation
126 East 32nd Street
San Francisco, CA 64892

Dear Ms Jenkins:

It is with considerable interest that I enclose my resume in response to your April 19th <u>Wall Street Journal</u> advertisement for a Human Resources Manager. This appears to be an exciting career opportunity, and I would welcome the chance to meet with you personally to discuss the contributions that I could make to your organization. I believe that my resume will attest to my strong credentials for this position.

Your ad states that you seek an advanced degree in Human Resources Management and 15 plus years as a Human Resources generalist in a major organization. You also require a skilled facilitator who is an advocate of participatory management principles and can lead senior management in developing new directions for the business.

I hold an M.S. in Industrial Relations from Michigan State and have had extensive training in Organization Development methodology. As Manager of Personnel for the Worster Corporation, a $565 million (12,000 employees) manufacturer of electronic components, I have broad responsibility for management of all Human Resources functions. I am a strong advocate of participatory management principles and currently serve as an internal O.D. consultant to senior management in their strategic panning efforts. I am considered to be a skilled facilitator of organizational change.

Addressing your required personal traits, I am frequently described by others as warm, friendly and outgoing. I have enjoyed excellent rapport with all levels of management and believe myself to be very open and approachable.

I believe that I am particularly well qualified for your position and would like to have the opportunity to meet with you to explore how I might contribute to the goals of your organization.

My salary requirements are in the mid-$80K range, and I can be reached during the evening at (216) 395-8876.

Thank you for your consideration, and I look forward to hearing from you.

Sincerely,

*Wilbur S. Stanton*

Wilbur S. Stanton

wrs

# COST ACCOUNTANT

A leading company in the manufacture of industrial heat exchangers, Kelso Corporation is seeking a Manufacturing Cost Accountant for its Lawndale plant. This position reports to the Plant Accounting Manager and is responsible for all brand cost accounting for the Big Bend line of industrial blowers. This is a challenging position with excellent career advancement opportunity. Kelso's sales have tripled in the last five years, and major expansion is planned.

We seek an experienced Cost Accountant with a B.S. in Accounting and at least 2 years of manufacturing cost experience. Prefer experience in metal fabrication facility; however, this is not a requirement. Should be thoroughly versed in standard cost methodology and Lotus 1-2-3. Must be computer literate and able to use IBM PC.

Excellent salary and fringe benefits provided.

Send resume in confidence to:

Conwell R. Leinbach
Employment Manager
Kelso Corporation
1325 Wexler Street
Philadelphia, PA 19113

An Equal Opportunity Employer

126 Beaker Street
Lynne, PA 19874
April 14, 1994

Mr. Conwell R. Leinbach
Employment Manager
Kelso Corporation
1325 Wexler Street
Philadelphia, PA 19113

Dear Mr. Leinbach:

I am forwarding my resume in response to your April 14th ad in
the <u>Philadelphia Inquirer</u> for a Cost Accountant. I am very much
interested in this position, and would appreciate your
consideration as a candidate.

You will note from the enclosed resume that I have many of the
attributes that you are seeking for this position. Please
consider the following:

1. B.S. in Accounting from the University of Pennsylvania
2. 3 years manufacturing cost accounting experience with
   Deltar Corporation, a fabricator of air conditioning
   cabinets
3. Currently apply standard manufacturing cost methodology
   to all brand costing for the Alpine line of industrial
   air conditioners
4. Thoroughly versed in use of Lotus and IBM PC

I am a hard worker who is noted for accuracy and timeliness. My
performance evaluations have consistently been at the "above
average" and "outstanding" level, and I can furnish excellent
references should you need them.

I would be pleased to have the opportunity to discuss this
position with you during a personal interview, and hope that you
will view my candidacy favorably.

I can be reached during the day, on a confidential basis, at
(215) 344-2773 or during evening hours at (215) 877-2525.

Thank you for your consideration, and I hope to be hearing from
you in the near future.

Sincerely,

*Alice J. Stockman*

Alice J. Stockman

sam

Enclosure

# BUYER — INDUSTRIAL CHEMICALS

National Foam, an industry leader and $875 million manufacturer of polyurethane foams for industrial applications, seeks a Buyer - Industrial Chemicals for its Corporate Procurement function. This position reports to the Vice President of Logistics and manages three Assistant Buyers in the annual procurement of some $125 million of raw material chemicals. This is a centralized buying function serving 5 manufacturing plants.

We seek an experienced industrial chemicals buyer with a B.S. degree in the sciences and at least 10 years experience in the purchase of bulk industrial chemicals. Must be skilled in the negotiation of long-term bulk contracts with a demonstrated record of cost savings and reputation for maintaining high quality and on-time delivery. Experience in purchase of TDI or resins or related chemicals helpful, but not required. Must be experienced with bulk purchasing and multi-location delivery of industrial chemicals.

Excellent compensation and benefits package is available for qualified candidates. Relocation assistance will also be provided.

Interested persons should send their resume to:

Jeffrey A. Morse
Director of Human Resources
National Foam, Inc.
123 Henderson Road
Old Forge, NY 89573

We are an Equal Opportunity Employer (M/F)

1200 Pine Tree Lane
Utica, New York 36729
November 8, 1993

Mr. Jeffrey A. Morse
Director of Human Resources
National Foam, Inc.
123 Henderson Road
Old Forge, NY 89573

Dear Mr. Morse:

Your November 2nd ad in the <u>Utica Times </u>for a Buyer - Industrial
Chemicals caught my eye. This position appears to fit my current
requirements exceptionally well, and I am therefore submitting my
resume for your consideration. I appear to be well qualified for
this position, and I am very interested in pursuing this
opportunity with your company.

Review of your ad indicates that you are seeking a degreed
Chemical Buyer with at least 10 years experience in bulk purchase
of industrial chemicals for a multi-plant company. Further, you
require a skilled negotiator with reputation for cost savings,
quality and on-time delivery. You also state that experience in
the purchase of TDI and industrial resins would be helpful.

I hold a B.S. degree in Chemistry and have been employed as a
Chemical Buyer for the Buttal Corporation for the last 12 years.
In this capacity, I purchase over $85 million of industrial
chemicals annually for 3 manufacturing facilities. All of this is
purchased in bulk lot under long-term contracts, which I have
negotiated with very favorable terms for Buttal.

Through consolidation of plant purchases and renegotiation
of all bulk chemical contracts, I was able to realize a $1.5
million annual savings for the company. Additionally, in 12
years, I have only ever experienced two late deliveries. Both
were due to weather emergencies and were unavoidable. I have also
established stringent testing standards for all incoming raw
materials that have virtually assured the delivery of top quality
product.

I am very interested in this position and would appreciate the
opportunity to further discuss this matter during a face-to-face
interview. I feel that I can make a strong contribution to your
company.

Please feel free to contact me at (417) 899-7335 during the day
or at (417) 977-2255 in the evening.

I would be pleased to hear from you. Thank you for your
consideration.

Sincerely,

*Scott M. Beatty*

Scott M. Beatty

atr

# 10

## OTHER EMPLOYMENT LETTERS

In past chapters, we have covered in detail the most commonly used cover letters. These include the general broadcast cover letter, the executive search cover letter, and the cover letter responding to employment advertisements. These categories make up some 80 to 90 percent of all cover letters written by job seekers.

There are some other less frequently used, but nonetheless important, employment letters with which you must also be familiar if you are going to run an effective job search campaign. Specifically, these are:

1. The résumé letter
2. The employment networking letter
3. The thank you letter

This final chapter will deal with these letters, discussing the purpose of each and providing some samples for your consideration and use.

## The Résumé Letter

The résumé letter is not a true cover letter—that is, a letter of transmittal for your employment résumé. Instead, it is intended to replace the résumé and to convey sufficient information about your background to create employer interest in interviewing you.

In general, I am not particularly fond of the résumé letter and do not recommend its use. It is usually a poor substitute for the résumé itself, and thus can frequently do the job seeker a great injustice if not properly designed. Specifically, if it is poorly planned and written, it does not provide sufficient information (when compared to the résumé) for the employer to make a reasonable assessment of the applicant's qualifications and for deciding whether to grant an interview. Additionally, it may frustrate the prospective employer by not providing sufficient detail, suggesting that the applicant is simply too lazy to prepare a proper summary of qualifications. Neither of these reactions will serve your cause very well.

It appears that the most frequent use of the résumé letter is by top-level corporate executives who wish simply to convey their availability and conduct a very cursory search of the job market. Generally, such letters are directed at the highest level of the target organization (usually Board Chairman, President, or Chief Executive Officer) and are intended to convey availability and general interest in discussing appropriate

163

opportunities. The typical logic supporting such letters is that the applicant's current position and employer "speak for themselves," and thus there is little need for a detailed résumé.

Although this can be true, it is not typically the case. Obviously, if the individual is a top corporate or division-level officer of a Fortune 200 company, use of a résumé letter may be sufficient. Suffice it to say, however, that if the applicant is the Chief Financial Officer of a little-known $20 million company, the résumé letter will not have quite the same effect, and its use may seem somewhat presumptuous (if used in the place of a formal résumé). In such a case, I strongly recommend a full résumé and conventional cover letter.

The use of the résumé letter by lesser-known top executives, middle managers, and professionals is not recommended. Since employer's name and position title convey little information to the reader in such cases, much more needs to be written to convey the same understanding about the author's background and responsibilities. The danger here, of course, is that the letter will become unwieldy and will therefore not be read by its recipient.

So, in summary, my advice is to use the résumé letter only in those cases where you are employed in a fairly high-level executive capacity with a well-known, major corporation or prestigious organization. Otherwise, the conventional cover letter and résumé will truly better serve your interests.

The following are some examples of résumé letters for use by key executives of well-known, prestigious organizations.

126 Biddle Lane
Wayne, PA 19285
August 21, 1992

Mr. Robert P. Stanton
Chairman of the Board
Brennon Petroleum Corporation
1800 East 42nd Street
New York, NY 29384


Dear Mr. Stanton:

Some recent changes in Board membership at National Corporation
have caused me to rethink career plans. I have therefore decided
to confidentially explore opportunities outside of the company. I
am sure you can appreciate the sensitivity of this matter.

As Senior Vice President of Operations for National Corporation,
I report to the President and am responsible for all operations
of the company. This entails managing 6 operating divisions (23
plants), 32,000 employees and an Operations budget of $5.2
billion. I have an excellent track record, including documentable
annual savings in the $1.2 billion range as the result of major
programs that I have implemented over the past 5 years.

I hold an M.B.A. from the Harvard Business School and have over
20 years of experience in manufacturing and operations
management.

My education and professional experience have well prepared me
for senior-level management assignments, and I am looking to
further expand my horizons.

Should you be aware of an appropriate opportunity or have some
thoughts about persons with whom I should be in contact, I would
appreciate your counsel. I can be reached at (316) 874-9959.

Thank you for your assistance in this matter.

Sincerely,

Phillip R. Strong

adm

135 Willsboro Blvd.
Devonshire, IL 19284
August 21, 1993


Ms Ruth A Crumpton
President
United Foods Corporation
825 Commerce Blvd.
Chicago, IL 19870


Dear Ms Crumpton:

I have recently decided to effect a career change and am now
confidentially exploring employment opportunities at the senior
level in general management. This search is being conducted on a
highly confidential basis, since my current company is not yet
aware of this decision.

I am a graduate of the University of Chicago with an M.B.A. in
Finance. My undergraduate training was at Cornell University,
where I earned a B.S. in Mechanical Engineering.

Currently, I am President of Kelsy Food Company, a $380 million
subsidiary of Great National Corporation. In this capacity, I
report directly to William Thornton, President of Great National,
and have total P&L responsibility for this 6,000-employee food
processing company. I also sit on the Board of Great National, a
position that I have held for 6 years.

The prospects for growth to senior-level corporate management are
not particularly encouraging for the foreseeable future. All
senior-level corporate officers are relatively young, and there
is no major business expansion planned over the next several
years. At age 38, I feel I must move on if I am going to realize
my longer-term career goals.

Ms Crumpton, as a leading executive of one of the Nation's major
food companies, should you be aware of a suitable senior-level
management opportunity, I would very much appreciate hearing from
you.

I can be reached at (812) 398-1837.

Thank you for your assistance in this matter.

Sincerely,

*Richard F. Brightson*

Richard F. Brightson

sar

## Employment Networking Letter

As most seasoned employment and outplacement professionals will tell you, personal networking is the most productive method for finding a job. Although estimates vary, it is generally agreed that a very high percentage of jobs are filled in this fashion—generally, this is thought to be in the neighborhood of 70 percent.

The reason for the unusually high success rate of employment networking is simple—personal contact. The term "employment networking" has come to mean the process by which one reaches out to a group of friends and acquaintances for their ongoing support during the job hunting process. These individuals are asked by the job seeker to give their direct support by providing job leads and referrals, as well as introductions to others who can provide similar support.

An important element of successful employment networking is known as "sourcing." Sourcing is a method by which one multiplies his or her personal contacts manyfold by "sourcing" immediate friends and acquaintances for the names of people who might assist in the job hunting campaign. These second-level contacts are then also "sourced" for the names of other people who may be of help. And so goes the networking chain, like cell division, multiplying the job searcher's initial personal contacts many times over, until the inevitable happens—employment!

Key to this networking process is the employment networking letter. The networking process normally calls for using this letter to accomplish two things:

1.  Set the stage for a personal introduction
2.  Transmit your résumé

It is thus very important to the success of the networking plan.

The mechanics of the networking process work as follow. First, ask a friend or acquaintance for the names of others who might help in making contacts as part of your job search. Make sure the friend or acquaintance has given permission for you to use his or her name when introducing yourself to this new contact. Then send an employment networking letter to this new contact asking for assistance with your job search. Include a copy of your résumé with the letter and ask the new contact to review it. Get in touch with the new contact, either personally or by phone, to determine if he or she is aware of any employment opportunities that are appropriate for you. Also ask to be introduced to others who may be able to assist you.

Thus, the employment networking letter is a vital link in the networking chain. It serves to set the stage for your personal introduction and to solicit help from others in your job search campaign.

Review of the sample letters at the end of this section of the chapter will show that effective employment networking letters contain certain key components. These are:

1. Personal opening

   a. Name of person making the referral
   b. Relationship to you
   c. Some personal comments (where appropriate)

2. Explanation of how referral occurred (optional)
3. Reason for job change (optional)
4. Reference to known position opening (if it exists)
5. Indirect approach (where no known opening exists)
6. Reference to enclosed résumé
7. Action statement to initiate personal contact (i.e., meeting or phone call)
8. Thank you

If carefully written, the employment networking letter can be a very effective tool. It makes use of personal ties and relationships to substantially expand your circle of contacts, directly involving legions of others in your job hunting campaign and opening numerous doors that would otherwise be closed to you. Since the employment networking letter sets the stage for these valuable introductions, it is important that it be well-written.

The following pages contain sample employment networking letters. They can be used to model similar letters for your use.

915 Mockingbird Lane
Wilshire, NH 18274
February 12, 1994

Mr. James F. Samuels
Vice President of Marketing
Vellar Corporation
22 Liberty Avenue
Boston, MA 13884

Dear Mr. Samuels:

Doug Robson, a close friend of mine, suggested that I contact
you. Doug and I have adjoining slips at Snuggsound Harbor, where
we have spent many summer weekends sailing together. I understand
that you enjoy a bit of sailing as well.

Last week, while at Knatts Marina, I mentioned to Doug that I had
decided to make a career move. Since my background is Sales and
Marketing, Doug suggested that I might want to contact you to see
if you might have any thoughts on this matter. Any ideas or
suggestions that you might have would be very much appreciated.

As you can see from the enclosed resume, I have an M.B.A. in
Marketing from Penn State University and over 20 years in the
Sales and Marketing field. Most recently, I have been National
Sales Manager for Wheaton Laboratories, a hazardous waste
engineering consulting firm. Unfortunately, Wheaton has been sold
to a group of private investors who will be installing their own
management team.

According to Doug, your firm is in the hazardous waste treatment
field. Perhaps you may be aware of someone who is currently
looking for a national sales or marketing manager. If not,
perhaps you can suggest some key contacts in the hazardous waste
treatment field with whom I should be in contact. Either way, I
would appreciate any thoughts or ideas you might have on this
matter.

I am planning to be in Boston the week beginning March 6th. If
your schedule permits, perhaps we could meet for lunch or dinner
and discuss this matter further. I will call your office early
next week to see if we can get together.

Thank you for your help, Mr. Samuels, and I look forward to the
possibility of meeting with you personally.

Sincerely,

*Winston B. Peters*

Winston B. Peters

adk

Enclosure

213 Orlando Road
Macon, GA 39184
August 26, 1989

Ms Dawn M. Marks
Director of Research
Braughn Laboratories
144 Technology Drive
Atlanta, GA 15728

Dear Dawn:

It appears that we have a close mutual friend. John Davidson and
I go back a few years. We were fraternity brothers at Bucknell
University and are now tennis partners in a group that has played
together for better than ten years. My wife, Sandra, and I get
together with the Davidsons for dinner on a regular basis. In
fact, although we have never met personally, both John and
Barbara have spoken of you often.

During dinner last Friday, I mentioned to John that I was
seriously considering a career change. It appears that my career
at Dennison Research Laboratories has pretty much plateaued.
Recent cuts in research funding by several of our key clients has
seriously dampened prospects for future growth opportunities, and
I have reluctantly concluded that I will need to move on.

I understand from John that Braughn Laboratories may be
contemplating an expansion and may be in the market for a
Principal Scientist in Absorbant Research. If this is the case,
my background may be of possible interest. I have a Ph.D. in
Materials Science and over 12 years advanced research in
absorbancy concepts. This has included some 16 patents in the
field. Perhaps you are familiar with some of my work. If not, I
have taken the liberty of enclosing a resume for your reference.

I am planning a trip to Atlanta in the next few weeks and would
appreciate the opportunity to meet with you. Perhaps we could
meet to mutually explore the possibility of employment with your
company. If my background is not an appropriate fit for your
anticipated requirements, however, Dawn, perhaps you would be
kind enough to offer your thoughts concerning my current job
hunting campaign. Your counsel would be greatly appreciated.

I will contact your office during this coming week to determine
an appropriate time for us to meet. Perhaps we could meet over
dinner.

I look forward to the prospect of meeting you personally, and
thank you for your assistance with my career change.

Sincerely,

Michael T. English

adm

Enclosure

## The Thank You Letter

No book on cover and employment letters could possibly be complete without mention of the thank you letter. As an employment professional, I have never ceased to be amazed at how employment candidates never think to send a basic thank you letter to prospective employers following an interview. If I had to estimate, I would say that fewer than 20 percent of employment candidates bother to extend this basic courtesy.

As an employment candidate, you should stop to consider that not only does the thank you letter show that you are appreciative of people's time and effort on your behalf, but (from the purely commercial standpoint) if well-constructed, it is an excellent opportunity to again market your skills and interest in the position. Why not take full advantage of it!

Review of the sample thank you letters at the end of this chapter will reveal the following basic components:

1.  Statement of appreciation for the interview
2.  Expression of interest in employment
3.  Reaffirmation of your qualifications for the position
4.  Final "thank you"

The following letters have incorporated these elements and are presented for your reference. I hope they will serve as effective models for designing your own post-interview thank you letter.

# SAMPLE E *Thank You Letter*

115 Juniper Road
Mobile, AL 18736
May 2, 1990

Ms Linda G. Baker
Director of Employment
National Chemical Company
120 Erie Road
Sandusky, OH 29847

Dear Ms Baker:

I wanted to let you know how much I appreciated the opportunity
to interview with National Chemical for the position of Principal
Scientist in Absorbant Technology. This is an exciting position,
and I want to reaffirm my strong interest in this assignment.

In particular, I enjoyed meeting Jane Johnston, Davis Keller and
Michael Ortz, and appreciated their time in explaining the
position of Principal Scientist and the function of Absorbant
Technology to me. This was most enlightening and served to peak
my interest in working as part of this group.

I feel that my Ph.D. in Materials Science and 6 years of
experience in absorbancy research with Dixon Laboratories should
serve me well in meeting the requirements of your position.
Additionally, I feel that my strong background in polymer
chemistry should prove very additive to the Group's efforts.

Again, Ms Baker, I appreciated the opportunity to visit with you.
Thank you for your hospitality, and I look forward to hearing
from you concerning the outcome of our discussions.

Sincerely,

*Garth R. Carter*

Garth R. Carter

mmg

## SAMPLE F *Thank You Letter*

400 East 7th Street
Lansdale, PA 19775
October 30, 1993

Mr. William A. Stanton
Director of Operations
Randsome Corporation
100 East Mountain Road
Denver, CO 18776

Dear Bill:

I wanted to thank you for the opportunity to interview for the
position of Purchasing Manager at Randsome Corporation. This
sounds like an exciting position, and I look forward to the
prospects of joining the company.

I particularly enjoyed our discussion concerning the application
of JIT to control of raw material costs. As you know, this can be
a highly effective tool. The work that I did in this area at
Wasser Company has resulted in approximate annual savings of over
$2 million. I feel that this could well be applied with success
in your organization, and would welcome the opportunity to lead
this effort.

As you know from our discussions, I am fully trained in
statistical process control techniques and total quality
concepts. Using these methods, the vendor certification program
that I have implemented at Wasser has been highly successful and
has been credited with reducing waste by nearly 90 percent. I
sensed your interest in this area, and believe this is another
area for opportunity at Randsome.

Needless to say, I am very interested in the position of
Purchasing Manager and would welcome an employment offer from
you. I feel that, with my overall qualifications and desire, I
could contribute significantly to your company.

Thank you again for the visit, and I look forward to hearing from
you shortly.

Sincerely,

*Carolyn A. Criswell*

Carolyn A. Criswell

dar

# INDEX